TWO LENINS

Hau
BOOKS

www.haubooks.com

THE MALINOWSKI MONOGRAPHS

In tribute to the foundational, yet productively contentious, nature of the ethnographic imagination in anthropology, this series honors the creator of the term "ethnographic theory" himself. Monographs included in this series represent unique contributions to anthropology and showcase groundbreaking work that contributes to the emergence of new ethnographically-inspired theories or challenge the way the "ethnographic" is conceived today.

TWO LENINS
A BRIEF ANTHROPOLOGY OF TIME

Nikolai Ssorin-Chaikov

Hau Books
Chicago

© 2017 Hau Books and Nikolai Ssorin-Chaikov

Cover, © 1923. Electric light bulb of a half-watt 1000 *svechi*, with a filament in the shape of V. I. Lenin. Courtesy of the Central Museum of Contemporary History of Russia.

Cover and layout design: Sheehan Moore

Typesetting: Prepress Plus (www.prepressplus.in)

ISBN: 978-0-9973675-3-9
LCCN: 2017934091

Hau Books
Chicago Distribution Center
11030 S. Langley
Chicago, IL 60628
www.haubooks.com

Hau Books is printed, marketed, and distributed by The University of Chicago Press.
www.press.uchicago.edu

Printed in the United States of America on acid-free paper.

Table of Contents

Acknowledgments   ix

List of figures   xi

CHAPTER 1
"You will be as Gods"   1

CHAPTER 2
Lenin and the combined fodder   19

CHAPTER 3
An American in Moscow   39

CHAPTER 4
Time for the field diary   69

CHAPTER 5
Hobbes' gift   95

CHAPTER 6
Modernity as time   121

References   131

Index   145

Acknowledgements

This book is the product of multiple anthropological temporalities. Its biography bridges two main areas of my academic interests: Siberian studies, where I have been involved since my initial fieldwork in Siberia in the late 1980s; and research into gift giving to Soviet leaders, which I have conducted since the early 2000s. The topic of time has been important for both. This book has developed as a conceptual sequel to an article on the *heterochrony* of Stalin's 70th birthday gifts, in 1949. In Siberia, I focused on deferral, delay, and teleological temporalities of Russian and Soviet statehood among indigenous Evenki. However, I first thought of combining these two kinds of material in a comparative and theoretical argument about temporal multiplicity when Victor Vakhstayn invited me to give a keynote address at the conference "Future as culture: Prognoses, representations, scenarios" at Moscow School of Social and Economic Sciences (2010). I am grateful to Laura Bear, who ran a seminar series, "Conflicts in time: Rethinking 'contemporary' globalization" (2008–11), in which I took part; she suggested that this might be a book-length project. I presented versions of this book's argument at London School of Economics, Russian University for the Humanities, University of Pennsylvania, University of Helsinki, University of Ekaterinburg, National Research University Higher School of Economics, and European University at St. Petersburg. In following the American Anthropological Association's Code of Ethics, I have anonymized the names of my informants and fieldwork locations. This project would not have been possible without the hospitality and collaboration of residents of the Siberian village that I call Katonga as well as the support by the Russian Foundation for Basic

Research, Division of Humanities and Social Sciences (Grant 15-01-00452 "Anthropology of the market and social transformations among Indigenous peoples of the north"). It would be equally impossible without research and curatorial collaboration with Olga Sosnina, particularly on the exhibition *Gifts to Soviet leaders* (Moscow 2006). Some of the viewers of this exhibition kindly consented to be interviewed, and many more left rich commentary in the exhibition response book, which became one of this project's sources. At various stages of work on this book I have also benefitted from intellectual exchanges on its themes and arguments with Alexander Semyonov, Alexei Vasiliev, Andrey Menshikov, Bruce Grant, Caroline Humphrey, Catriona Kelly, Greg Yudin, François-Xavier Nérard, Kevin Platt, Maria Loskutova, Mikhail Boytsov, Paolo Heywood, Peter Holquist, Sarah Green, Stephan Feuchtwang, Theodor Shanin, Timo Kaartinen, the late Tod Hartman, Vadim Radaev, and Vyacheslav Ivanov. I am grateful to the anonymous reviewers of this book's manuscript and to Alex Skinner, Heather Paxson, and Stefan Helmreich for thorough and insightful engagement with this text as a whole.

List of figures

Figure 1. Sculptural composition, *Eritis sicut deus*, by Hugo Wolfgang Rheinhold, circa 1893. Gift to V. I. Lenin from American businessman Armand Hammer, October 1921. *Courtesy of the Museum of Lenin's Flat and Study, Gorki Leninskie.*

Figure 2. Electric light bulb of a half-watt 1000 *svechi*, with a filament in the shape of V. I. Lenin. Gift to the 12th Congress of the Russian Communist Party (Bolsheviks) from the workers of the First and Second United Electric Lamp Factory, April 23, 1923. *Courtesy of the Central Museum of Contemporary History of Russia.*

Figure 3. "American business leaders in Lenin's Kremlin study," 1964. *Soviet Life Magazine.*

Figure 4. "To Lenin who first wrote down the great unwritten laws, with great admiration." Dedication of Henri Barbusse of his *Le lueur dans l'abime [The glow in the abyss]* (Paris 1920), as a gift to V. I. Lenin. *Courtesy of the Museum of Lenin's Flat and Study, Gorki Leninskie.*

Figure 5. "To Vladimir Il'ich Ulianov (Lenin), Who mightily moved hard forest reality into dream [tale]." Dedication of Ivan Kasatkin of his *Forest true stories* (Moscow 1919), as a gift to V. I. Lenin. *Courtesy of the Museum of Lenin's Flat and Study, Gorki Leninskie.*

Figure 6a–i. China set with the motifs of P. P. Bazhov's tale, "Warrior's mitten." Gift to I. V. Stalin for his 70th birthday from the collective of the Baranovo Porcelain Factory, 1949. *Courtesy of the Central Museum of Contemporary History of Russia.*

Figure 7a, b. Book cover of Armand Hammer's *The quest of the Romanoff treasure.* New York: W. F. Payson, 1932; and cup from china set with the motifs of P. P. Bazhov's tale, "Warrior's mitten." Gift to I. V. Stalin for his 70th birthday from the collective of the Baranovo Porcelain Factory, 1949. *Courtesy of the Central Museum of Contemporary History of Russia.*

Figure 1. Sculptural composition, *Eritis sicut deus*, by Hugo Wolfgang Rheinhold, circa 1893. Gift to V. I. Lenin from American businessman Armand Hammer, October 1921. *Courtesy of the Museum of Lenin's Flat and Study, Gorki Leninskie.*

CHAPTER I

"You will be as gods"

March on, my land, move on, my land,
The commune is at the gates!
Forward, time!
Time—forward!
—Vladimir Mayakovski, "The march of time"

"What day is it?" asked Pooh.
"It's today," squeaked Piglet.
"My favorite day," said Pooh.
—A. A. Milne, *Winnie-the-Pooh*

An ape sits on the works of Darwin, holding a drawing compass with the toes of one of its feet over the pages of an open book. The ape contemplates a skull, which it holds in its right hand (see fig. 1). The Latin inscription on the open page of the book reads, "You will be as gods" (*Eritis sicut deus*). These words, which gave the figurine its title, come from Genesis 3:5: "But God knows that in the day that you eat of [the fruit of the tree, which is among the paradise], your eyes will open and you will be as gods, knowing good and evil [*scientes bonum et malum*]." This figurine is Hugo Wolfgang Rheinhold's, circa 1893. It is a bronze cast, 32.4 centimeters high, which exists in a number of copies.

The inscription, while Biblical, nonetheless denotes a message that is resolutely secular. It gives us a "Darwinian plot" (Beer 2000), which made this figurine a popular collection item in the early twentieth century in the world of biology and medicine. Its casts are on display at the Boston Medical Library, the University of Edinburgh's Institute of Evolutionary Biology, the Aberdeen Medico-Chirurgical Society, the Medical Library of Queen's University, Canada, and many more places (cf. Richter and Schmetzke 2007). But the particular cast of which I write here is in an unlikely location. It holds pride of place in the Museum of the Kremlin's Flat of Vladimir Lenin. Lenin received it as a gift from a young American businessman, Armand Hammer, who visited him in 1921. As a gift, the figurine received an unintended, yet well-fitting, Marxist meaning: "You will be as gods," the inscription seems to say, in building a new and radically different society.

Whether it represents a triumph of natural science or socialism, the *Eritis sicut deus* sculpture presents a temporal narrative—in fact, several narratives, each held in a mirror reflection of the others. The main narrative is one of Darwinian time. This biological time of evolution inverts another temporality, Christian, since what the sculpture represents is not a fall from Eden but rather an ascent of Man. At first glance, this all meshes well with Marxist historical materialist time. But in this context, Darwinian time is not just reflected in—or aligned with—Marxist time but rather split into two temporalities: biological and social. As Friedrich Engels famously stated, "just as Darwin discovered the law of development of organic nature, so Marx discovered the law of development of human history" (Engels 1989: 467). But Marxism rejected social Darwinism as the "bourgeois ideology" par excellence that naturalizes capitalist market relations. Equally famously, Engels observes that

> The whole Darwinian theory of the struggle for life is simply the transference from
> society to organic nature of Hobbes' theory of *bellum omnium contra omnes* [the war
> of each against all], and of the bourgeois economic theory of competition, as well
> as the Malthusian theory of population. When once this feat has been accom-
> plished . . . , it is very easy to transfer these theories back again from natural history
> to the history of society, and altogether too naïvely to maintain that thereby these
> assertions have been proved as eternal natural laws of society. (Engels 1991: 107–8)

In Marxist perspective, social Darwinism does not just give a social version of the biological evolutionary time. It de-temporalizes a particular version of capitalist modernity as "eternal natural laws."

But the sculpture itself refers only to Christianity and Darwinism. The Marxist temporality is manifested in this item only because this particular cast is a gift to Lenin. This gift act further complicates the canvass of temporalities of *Eritis sicut deus*, as it is not just the Marxist temporality that is added to the picture but also the *time of the gift*. As a part of the display of the Museum of the Lenin's Kremlin Flat, the statue stands for a distinctly Soviet understanding of gift reciprocity that links the very concept of socialist modernity—the new dawn of history, in which "You will be as gods"—with the grateful world to which this modernity is given. In this perspective, Hammer's figurine is a countergift. But this gift time is itself complex: its circular reciprocity is about a *gift of the new time* that "marches" toward the commune that is already "at the gates" (to quote Vladimir Mayakovski's poem, "The march of time").

***

Time—in anthropological perspective—is a culturally specific construct that combines ways of structuring daily activities with broader meanings about the past, present, and future. The case of Hammer's gift and his relations with Lenin and the Soviet Union condenses several meanings of time. They are culturally specific to early twentieth-century modernity, including Marxism. In fact, we see how his gift makes visible multiple and contested meanings of *modernity* through multiple and contested meanings of *time*. Modernity has long been understood as producing a homogeneous time that is "uniform, infinitely divisible, and continuous" (Sorokin and Merton 1937: 616). Indeed, one of the first things the Soviet government did after the revolution was to adopt the Gregorian calendar, thereby eliminating a two-week time difference with the Julian calendar that Russia had previously followed. Doing so integrated Russia into the emergent frameworks of standard global time (Conrad 2016; Ogle 2015). But this immediately complicated Soviet revolutionary chronology. The storming of the Winter Palace on October 23, 1917—which marked the start of Bolshevik Revolution and quickly became the major Soviet holiday, the "Day of October Revolution"—according to the new calendar was to be celebrated on November 7. Settling on a global, shared territory of calendar time (although see Gumerova [n.d.] on Soviet calendar experiments such as the five-day week and rotating holidays), Soviet time then moved to make a claim to a radical difference in terms of something else: the time that is *epochal*. In this new epochal time, it hardly mattered that the "Day of October Revolution" was in

November. Rather than being purely chronological, this epochal time mapped history and humanity through a new time of socialist modernity. It started with the October Revolution as a new dawn of history, celebrated by statements such as Mayakovski's "March of time" or material objects like an electric light bulb with a filament in the shape of Lenin (see fig. 2).

But in the early 1920s, when Hammer visited Lenin, these new times of energetic socialist futurism coexisted with the equally energetic capitalism of Lenin's New Economic Policies. Hammer was instrumental in this turn to capitalism and benefited from it personally. Indeed, perhaps his gift to Lenin turned out, rather, to be a ricocheting gift to Hammer who subsequently made a business empire out of contacts with the Soviet Union. Perhaps this very statue was a business gift and followed the reciprocal temporality of business, rather than gifts. Moreover, given the importance of American business concessions, which Lenin discussed with Hammer during his audience, and of Fordism, which Lenin took as a model for Soviet industrialization, this sculpture may equally problematize who is giving gifts of new time and to whom. The inscription— "You will be as gods"—may well stand for the gift of American modernity to Russia, rather than the Russian revolutionary gift to the world.

***

The reader must now be persuaded that the many meanings of time of modernity that this gift articulates and in fact celebrates can be expanded almost to infinity. But my aim here is not to ask how many angels can dance on the head of a pin. It is well established that sociocultural time is multiple. Ethnographic inquiry no longer proceeds by assuming either a universal singularity of time or its cultural singularity within a given society as an isolated unit—for example, the Nuer or Balinese time (Evans-Pritchard 1940; Geertz 1966). Anthropology acknowledges composite and hierarchically assembled temporalities of most of the phenomena that it explores. It is not just that empire or nation, state socialism, or global capitalism constitutes multiple temporalities. Each of their "parts"—the temporalities of the market, governance, consumption, reproduction, work, politics, etc.—are in turn intrinsic multiplicities (cf. Abu-Shams and González-Vázquez 2014; Bear 2014; Bestor 2001; Birth 2012; Chelcea 2014; Dick 2010; Franklin 2014; Greenhouse 1996; Lazar 2014; May and Thrift 2003; Miyazaki 2003; Rosenberg and Grafton 2010; Rowlands 1995; Shove, Trentmann, and Wilk 2009; Verdery 1996; Wengrow 2005).

Figure 2. Electric light bulb of a half-watt 1000 *svechi*, with a filament in the shape of V. I. Lenin. Gift to the 12th Congress of the Russian Communist Party (Bolsheviks) from the workers of the First and Second United Electric Lamp Factory, April 23, 1923. *Courtesy of the Central Museum of Contemporary History of Russia.*

My own moment of "discovering" temporal multiplicity occurred when I explored a single event: Joseph Stalin's birthday of 1949. I did it through the lens of a single practice of birthday gift giving and an institutional singularity of the exhibition of these gifts at the Pushkin Fine Arts Museum, Moscow, where these gifts displaced art—to the triumph of some and the horror of others—over the ten days leading up to the birthday celebration (Ssorin-Chaikov 2006a). I was interested in charting how the temporality of birthday gift giving was divisible into the temporality of the birthday and the gift, the conflicting eternities of the teleological time of socialism and of the high art, the geopolitical time of the Cold War, and the micromaterial time of exhibition construction and its entropy—with bottles of wine from French Communists arriving half-empty or exhibition draping accumulating moths and dangerous dampness before its display was completed. This is, indeed, but one example of sociocultural time appearing as a composite. As Nancy Munn put it, time is "divisible" not just by *culture* or *concepts* but by "action systems" or "systems of movement," each of which "produce[s] . . . its own time'" (Munn 1983: 280). Whatever is taken as a single "sociocultural time," it can be shown to contain "multiple dimensions" such as "sequencing, timing, past-present-future relations, etc." (Munn 1992: 116). The three questions that follow from this constitute this book's problematic.

Three questions

First, all this means that we are at a point when temporal multiplicity and complexity is hardly in need of another confirmation. The issue, rather, is where we go from here. Multiplicity and complexity are good questions, but they are poor answers if they come (as they so often do) without qualification as to how a given multiplicity is organized and what we can tell in addition to acknowledging that "X is complex and multiple." In this book, multiplicity is not a destination where an argument finally arrives but a point of departure. Once acknowledged, multiplicity immediately prompts questions about its composition: what exactly it is, how it is structured, and how different temporalities that are in it are interrelated.

The second question is how to conceptualize these relations between temporalities precisely *as relations*. This book's key proposition in regard to time is *relational* rather than relativist. What is important for me when considering, for example, *Eritis sicut deus*, is not that each of its Christian, Darwinist, Marxist, and gift temporalities constitute culturally distinct singularities. The issue is, rather, that each is what it is through the lens of others. We see Christian temporality through the Darwinian narrative, and Darwinian through the Marxist narrative. Together, they form a relationship that is itself specific to the time and place when these temporalities were articulated together—that is, Soviet Russia of the early 1920s.

Incidentally, it was at about the same time, in 1923, that Russian anthropologist Vladimir Bogoraz published what has become an important relativist statement in the anthropology of time. His book *Einstein and religion* opens with the premise that "each system S, each realm of phenomena, has its own space and its own time" (Bogoraz 1923: 4). This explicitly draws on relativity theory, but Bogoraz' move is characteristic of cultural relativism, which in the form of Boasian anthropology predates relativity theory. As early as in 1887, Franz Boas argued that "civilization is not something absolute, but that it is relative, and that our ideas and conceptions are true only so far as our civilization goes" (Boas 1974: 64). "System S" in Bogoraz' formulation stands for culture, that is, for a culturally specific belief system (shamanism is Bogoraz' prime concern): "it is only from this point of view we can interpret the measurement data in the religious sphere" (Bogoraz 1923; see Bogoras 1925 for an English-language summary of this perspective). Such a cultural system appears as an isolated universe that encapsulates its own difference—a uniquely structured timespace.

In contrast to cultural relativism, relativity theory takes this very difference to be relational, that is, a matter of a mutually constituted system of movement. It is grounded in the philosophical premise that time is not an essence but a relation. Time is not a substance that "flows" or an area that "begins" or "ends." It is not a thing but a relation between things. Anthropologists, Bogoraz included, have shared this premise in regard to sociocultural time. But this shared premise has different implications for perspectives that are relational and relativist. My question is how to extend the relational perspective to relations between temporalities, in addition to treating each individual temporality as a relation.

But this question is linked to a trickier issue. What is the status of temporal multiplicity in relation to what it describes—that is, to time? What does it actually mean to say that sociocultural time is multiple? When we say that something happened at the same time as something else, "at the same time" refers to the simultaneity of the two events. But how it is that a different *time* exists "at the same time"? My third question is precisely this: what is this "same time" in which others exist? In what way, if at all, does this "same time" constitute simultaneity? If so, what exactly is "simultaneity" in relation to different notions of time that it encompasses?

Two Lenins

This book's title refers to two different persons at the center of two kinds of material on which I draw in the discussion of these questions. One is the Soviet leader, Vladimir Lenin, whom readers will see receiving gifts from American businessman Armand Hammer in early 1920s Moscow. The other will take us to a very different territory, four time zones away from Moscow, to the north of the Siberian Krasnoyarsk province, where we will see an indigenous Evenki hunter, also named Vladimir and jokingly nicknamed "Lenin," living through late socialism and postsocialism.

The Evenki "Lenin" visited Lenin's Tomb in Moscow in the 1960s and received his nickname after that trip. But the book is not about this or any other encounter between the two Lenins, nor about their juxtaposition. This is not a study of Lenin's cult in Russia (cf. Dickerman 2001; Tumarkin 1987; Yurchak 2015). Chapters of this book do not add up to a "provincialized" (Chakrabarty 2000) exploration of the Russian and Soviet imperial space, although they include materials on its "central" and "remote" locations on an equal footing, nor are they episodes of the global history of the Soviet project, although some of the discussion links Russia and the United States. Some of this material is about the 1920s and other material is about the 1990s, but this book is not a cross-temporal comparison (cf. Armitage 2015). If anything, the book is brought together by the issue of Soviet modernity, and modernity more broadly. In chapters 5 and 6, I offer some conclusions about this. I suggest that while modernity is associated with the homogenized chronological time, it is important to approach it as a temporal multiplicity. I also suggest viewing modernity not merely as a distinct condition that has its own temporal organization but as itself a form of time. But these substantive observations are tentative. My primary goal in this book is, rather, to put forward a methodological argument. I ask not just what the multiple temporalities are at work in the cases of the two Lenins; I also ask how they are interrelated in each of them. My aim is to link the ethnographic questions of *how* (how to see relatedness in a temporal multiplicity? how does it work?) with the theoretical questions of *what* (that is, what about the implications of this relatedness for the understanding of the temporalities in question). Case studies about two Lenins highlight two different ways in which I suggest we can think about relatedness within a temporal multiplicity.

Change and exchange

This book is a thought experiment with two kinds of relationships between temporalities that I call *change* and *exchange*. Let me use the example of Hammer's gift to introduce them both. As we have already seen, in this particular instance, Christianity, Darwinism, and Marxism easily form a sequence of competing truth claims about time. *Change* (my first form of relatedness) here is not so much—and not just—a linear change assumed by these temporal frameworks. Rather, it is a change from one temporal framework to another in a way that renders a preceding framework untrue completely (e.g., Darwinism in regard to Christianity) or partially (e.g., Marxism splitting Darwinian time into biological and social).

These sequences are relations of rupture. Also, in this particular linear movement (change) from one temporality to another, these relations of change are at the same time the relations of truth. These *change* relations of truth are modernist in a broad sense of the term: they include both modernity's secular contexts and monotheistic background. A disagreement about the true meaning of time (whether it is Christian, Darwinist, or Marxist) is underpinned by a shared understanding that the truth, like God, is one (Yanagisako and Delaney 1995). Since this movement takes place on the grounds of the truth-value of each of these frameworks, to maintain one of them is possible only at the expense of the other: the temporality of the world was thought to be X but "in fact," as it turns out, it is not X but Y. The relation "X is in fact Y" is not equivalent to X = Y. The equation works only in one direction: X is revealed as Y. But that does not then mean that Y could be revealed as X. X is Y, but Y is not X. If these different frameworks coexist—as they do inscribed on the ape figurine—they form a hierarchy or chronotope (Bakhtin 1975) in which it is the transition "X is in fact Y" that is actually depicted. These are hierarchies of things that are true and those that are not at all, or less so. From the point of view of Marxist time in the composite aesthetics of *Eritis sicut deus*, it is this time that forms the top of a hierarchy of truth; Darwinian time is the next step down, while Christian time is at the bottom.

Exchange is another modality of relatedness between temporalities. Recall this gift's ambiguity. Perhaps it was a gift of gratitude to Lenin for Soviet

Russia's socialism as a gift to the world. Perhaps it was a token of the American gift of modernity to Russia. Perhaps this was a way to begin relations that led to Hammer's business empire. The point is, none of this is actually untrue. Each of these meanings is temporal, highlighting not just capitalist and socialist temporalities but also biographical temporalities of Lenin and Hammer, and the biography of Hammer's wealth. Hammer had communist sympathies, but this did not stop him from being a shrewd capitalist. Neither Marxism nor capitalism, neither Leninist Communist plans nor the Social-Darwinist jungle of the market is rendered false in this particular instance of giving. Rather, as I discuss in detail in chapter 3, each temporality is a resource for others. Each takes the other in, uses it, and absorbs it, without, however, transforming it into itself completely. To stress this difference, I call these relations of exchange (and not change). They substitute X with Y; in doing so, they displace X but do not erase it.

This *exchange* works very differently from *change*. As noted above, in *change*, when the temporality of the world was thought to be X, it turns out to be not X but Y. X is Y but Y is not X. In *exchange*, X = Y and Y = X. There is no linear progress from one meaning of time to the other; instead, there is a trade and an accumulation. Soviet Russia benefits from Hammer's gifts of capitalism and Hammer undoubtedly benefits from Soviet Russia. Exchange is a way to conceptualize temporalities that transpire when time is taken and time is given.

But, if *change* is a relation of unbridgeable difference, *exchange* is a relation of identity (X = Y), which nonetheless preserves difference. As Marx (1996) famously put it for economic exchange, if grain is exchanged for iron, there is something common in both, and in the same proportion. But if they really were equivalent, there would be no need for exchange. Marx himself sees this exchange through the lens of labor *time* that underscores each of these commodities. Abstract labor time is what is common, for Marx, in both grain and iron, and in the same proportion, while it is the concrete labor time of making grain and iron that is being exchanged. This Marxist analytic is useful here, but with a qualification that it is not merely something that explains, but something that needs explaining—it is one of the temporalities to be explored in a relationship of exchange with others. Now, let us think of Marxist time itself as exchanged for the time of social Darwinism, as in Lenin's complex exchanges with Hammer. There is something common there, and in the same proportion. But if these temporalities really were equivalent, there would be no need for exchange. Here, different temporalities are substituted and translated into one another, but not erased. Furthermore, each works as a measuring devise for the other. If, in Marx' example, grain is a measure of value for iron, and iron for the value of grain, here Marxist temporality is a measure of value for the time of social Darwinism. But unlike Marx's discussion, there is no real time that in fact underscores these exchanges, as labor time does for Marx in his understanding of the value of commodity. Marx' proposition of labor time would be a case in relations of *change* between temporalities in which one modality of time falsifies others, such as the temporalities of the market that do not just mask the labor time but also "eternalize" the "Darwinian theory of the struggle for life" (Engels 1991: 107) and require a Marxist description of the truth of these processes of alienation and naturalization. In contrast, *exchange* measures but it does not falsify. It just shows exactly how Marxism and social Darwinism are different, while change follows from one out of the two being false. These two forms of relations between temporalities, change and exchange, are detailed in chapter 2 and chapter 3.

Simultaneity

In what ways, if at all, does this multiplicity constitute simultaneity? What is the time in which these different times exist *at the same time*? One way to think about simultaneity is structural. For instance, consider Marcel Mauss' concept of "total" social phenomena, such as gifts, which express "*all at once and at a stroke all sorts of institutions*" that are "*at the same time*" religious, economic, political, familial, aesthetic, etc. (Mauss 2016: 59; emphasis added). In the case of meaning of time of Hammer's gift, the temporal multiplicity that it articulates could be a Maussian total social fact. To paraphrase Mauss, in this multiplicity, all kinds of temporalities of modernity are given expression *at the same time*: religious (Christian), scientific (Darwinist), economic (social-Darwinist), political (Marxist), etc. Although Mauss himself acknowledged that this is "multiplicity of social things in motion" (Mauss 2016: 59), simultaneity as a structural construct is itself out of time in his conceptualization of the gift, that is, it works by the omission of any detailed qualification of its own temporality. The structural timelessness of the simultaneity of total social fact seems to be the flip side of what Johannes Fabian (1983) critiqued: the timelessness of the ethnographic present, "the other time" in which the subjects of ethnography existed, distinct from linear and historical time of anthropology itself. "One and the same time" stands for the totality, and truth, of the perspective of the anthropologist as an outsider.

In chapter 4, I add my own research time to the temporalities that this book explores. While in this analytical move I am inspired by Fabian's critique of classical anthropological temporalities, it made me note the limitations of Fabian's own notion of simultaneity, which he terms as *coevalness*. Fabian develops it with the aim to counter structural, evolutionary, and relativist orderings of cultural multiplicity. His aim is to explore the ways in which assumptions about time enter the construction of objects of anthropological research. But while Fabian calls for anthropology "to meet the Other on the same ground, in the same Time" (1983: 165), he does not ask what this "same time" is. His describes this simultaneity merely as a "spatialization"—that is, as positioning differences, including differences between anthropologists and informants and, by implication, between different cultural models of time, "side by side." There are different articulations, frequencies, pitches, and tempos of interactions, he concludes, and all are contemporary. All these "dimensions of time" can and should be "transcribed as spatial relations" (Fabian 1983: 162–63).

But space, while good for cataloging, for putting things "side by side," is not necessarily good for conceptualizing dynamic relatedness. As Doreen Massey puts it, we can only imagine a spatial concept of simultaneity through a particular time—as if "an instant flashing of a pin-ball machine." This notion of space "is inadequate" precisely because it is also time (Massey 1992: 80). I argue that in order to understand simultaneity, we do need to incorporate space into the discussion of time, not in the sense of Fabian but following Henri Bergson (1965). However, this would not be in contradiction with Fabian's key thesis that the temporalities of the observer and the observed are on the par with each other. This, in fact, also incorporates Mauss, but only if we recall, following Claude Lévi-Strauss, that "to call the social fact total is not merely to signify that everything observed is part of the observation but also, and above all, that . . . the observer himself is a part of the observation" (Lévi-Strauss 1987: 29).

Bergson argues that our (that is, modern philosophical) conceptualization of time is spatial. We "spatialize time" when we think about it—we imagine it as a line or a circle. In this imagination, *instant* and *duration* are properties of space ("dot" and "line"). For Bergson, however, this space is not the physical space or "the same ground" as we saw with Fabian, where we "put side by side" cultural and temporal differences. Bergson's space is that of "time that is spatialized" as a matter of measurement. Time is measured through motion. But measurement is possible "because we are capable of performing motions ourselves and because these motions then have a dual aspect. As muscular sensation, they are a part of the stream of our conscious life, they endure; as visual perception, they describe a trajectory, *they claim a space*" (Bergson 1965: 50; emphasis added). For example, in order to measure time, we imagine it as a line.

The motion that we perform ourselves is "contemporaneous" with the motion with which we measure time. Motion is a relationship between at least two bodies, and thus it is already a matter of *simultaneity*:

> But, if we can correlate these two unwindings, it is only because we have at our disposal the *concept* of simultaneity; and we owe this concept to our ability to perceive external flows of events either together with the flow of our own duration, or separately from it, or, still better, both separately and together, *at one and the same time*. If we then refer to two external flows which take up the same duration as being "simultaneous," it is because they abide within the duration of yet a third, our own. (Bergson 1965: 51; emphasis added)

Bergson defines simultaneity as at least two instantaneous perceptions in the same mental act, out of which we should be able to make one or two "at will" (1965: 51). But we can have, he goes on to say, the idea of an "instant" as long as we are cable of converting time into space. Duration has no instants, while a line, a spatial representation of duration, is divisible into points.

"As soon as we make a line correspond to a duration, to portions of this line there must correspond 'portions of duration' and to an extremity of the line, an 'extremity of duration'; such as the instant—something that does not exist actually, but virtually" (Bergson 1965: 53). Bergson insists on the intuitive match between these perceptions and the world. For him, this is possible because these perceptions are already given to us in the shape of the world that we have. It is not just "entirely in our interest" to take a motion that is independent of the motion of our own body, consciousness and concepts for the "unfolding of time." "In truth, we find it already taken. Society has adopted it for us. It is the earth's rotational motion" (Bergson 1965: 51).

Bergson aims at a philosophical critique of relativity theory and insists that there are multiple "real" times, rather than the relativity of the single real time (cf. Canales 2015). However, in this book, what I have taken from this is not what anthropology has already taken for granted—for example, what is "real" is multiple. Rather, I am interested in thinking with Bergson's relatedness of motion—more precisely, the reciprocity of motion (cf. Bergson 1965: 75–79)—in order to "spatialize" conceptually not merely time but relatedness between different temporalities.

Benedict Anderson (1983) comes close to this when he proposes the notion of "homogeneous, empty time" as a particular kind of simultaneity that is central to nation as an imagined community. He speaks of "simultaneity-along-time" and simultaneity as "transverse, cross-time, marked not by prefiguring and fulfillment, but by temporal *coincidence*, and measured by clock and calendar" (1983: 24; emphasis added). Anderson discusses this simultaneity by drawing on Walter Benjamin and Erich Auerbach rather than Bergson. But it is possible to put this in Bergson's terms. These simultaneities-along-time are measuring devices, which enable temporalities to be perceived, via Bergson, either together or separately—"or, still better, both separately and together, *at one and the same time* (Bergson 1965: 51; emphasis added). This has been my point precisely when I proposed above that the Christian, Darwinist, Marxist, and gift temporalities of *Eritis sicut deus* mirror of each other, and in doing so they measure each other. This mirroring and measuring is exchange between them.

In turn, Tom Boellstorff (2007) queries the notion of coincidence. Boellstorff takes Indonesia as his point of departure (which was also Anderson's concern), focusing on the coincidences of discourses on the nation and sexuality, and develops his interpretive frame out of coincidences of these discourses and those of anthropology and queers studies. Boellstorff problematizes the notion of flow, which can include a taken-for-granted assumption of linear "straight" time. He "queers" this straight time from the point of view of oscillations and convergence of the temporalities of nation, sexuality, research, and activism (Boellstorff 2007: 26–32). He suggests that coincidence is, first, a moment when two or more temporal regimes meet, and, second, that it is a temporality of its own, rather than thinking of coincidence as something that happens within a singular, overarching time.

Temporal mapping

Simultaneity and coincidence, as Anderson and Boellstorff see them, are not categories of a universal philosophy of time, as they are for Bergson. They are empirical devices that account for cultural roots of nationalism (Anderson) or those of sexuality and desire as well as temporalities of Indonesian modernity and anthropology (Boellstorff). In this book, my goal is also similarly ethnographic. I am concerned with specific configurations of temporal multiplicity that are at work in socialist modernity. Here, I would like to make a leap from Bergson's "time that is spatialized" to Alfred Gell's "temporal mapping." Gell (1992) draws on J. M. E. McTaggart and the subsequent analytical philosophy of time that develops time-maps as the formal concept of temporal series "A" and "B." A-series are culturally or perceptually different notions of past, present, and future. B-series are categorizations of time according to whether they occur before or after one another. This before/after series "is just a row of events strung together, like the beads on a necklace" (Gell 1992: 151).

According to McTaggart (1908), the distinction between A- and B-series was subsequently appended by two camps of theorists that disagreed as to which of these two models of time is correct (cf. Prior 1957; Mellor 1998). For Gell, A-series are cultural constructs, or "perceptions" while B-series are their elementary units that are, in contrast, objective and "real," and reflect the temporal relationships between events "as they really are, out there." But, he argues, we do not have direct access to the B-series: "we know B-series time through temporal models [the A-series], which reflect the structure of B-series time without accessing it directly" (1992: 161, 240). Analytical philosophers may well disagree with this, depending on which camp they are in; and an anthropological objection would be to question who exactly the *we* are who draw a distinction between a cultural perception and reality. If *we* are anthropologists who can see elementary units of true time, we construct a hierarchy between scientific knowledge and cultural constructs. If *we* are all those who do not have direct access to the B-series, how do we know about it?

My own take on these questions is close to McTaggart's original notion. Both A- and B-series are perceptions or theories, but both are necessary: "It is essential to the reality of time that its events should form an A series as well as a B series" (McTaggart 1908: 458). But I apply the A- and B-series distinction differently. Temporalities that I discuss as examples here, such as the ones of Christianity, Darwinism, and Marxism can be described as an A-series. But *relations* of change and exchange between these temporalities that can be put in terms of the B-series: if Darwinism is true, and not Christianity, then Darwinism is after Christianity. In other words, the reason I turn to this particular language of description of time is that it is useful for developing a relational (and not relativist) perspective on temporal multiplicity. I apply the concept of B-series to sequences of competing truth claims about time. It is these sequences that can be categorized on the basis on what comes first and what comes second.

One of the problems that I consider below is an extent to which "exchange" may be characterized in terms of such B-series. The problem is that while B-series of time can be thought of as "a row of events strung together, like the beads on a necklace" (Gell 1992: 151), not all exchange can be imagined as a movement of a bead, as in a circular row of a rosary. The actual complexities of exchange relations between temporalities break the linearity of the B-series distinctions (see chapters 3 and 5). It is also important to acknowledge that the vocabulary of A- and B-series has formalist overtones, and so does my typology of change versus exchange. This suggests finding formal plots and stories, and is indeed close to the Russian formalism of Vladimir Propp and Victor Shklovski. But in what follows below, there will be very little formal plot analysis and no Bergson lines and dots. Instead of plots there will be narratives of change and exchange as descriptions of ethnographic situations. What I take from formalism is a broad interest in morphology in the sense of Goethe's, as it was used by Propp—that is, not so much assuming that "there is a single . . . type that runs through all organic creatures," but that "a theory of form is a theory of transformations" (Goethe cited in Propp 1968: 20, 80).

In addressing this question, it is instructive to keep in mind another cultural conceptualization of timespace that originated in the 1920s: Mikhail Bakhtin's notion of "chronotope" (which, as a term, also a borrows from Einstein). Bakhtin is widely credited for demonstrating that time and space constitute a narrative and cultural unity. But what is rarely acknowledged is that one of his key conclusions is that a single chronotope is likely to be a multiplicity. Internally, each "major" chronotope, he submits, contains a number of "minor" ones to the point that each literary motif in a novel is a chronotope of its own kind; further, and very importantly, each textual chronotope "extends" to external world. It exists *in a relation* to the chronotope of this text's performer, listener, and reader (Bakhtin 1975: 400–401)—and, by implication, as I will discuss in chapter 4 below, in relation to the chronotope of the scholar as a particular kind of listener and reader.

***

The book will unfold in the following chapters. Chapter 2, "Lenin and the combined fodder" will take us to a post-Soviet collective farm. I use a case of the disappearance of a load of combined fodder to illustrate the relations of change between a linear temporality of Soviet developmental time, cyclical rhythms of travel and infrastructure, and a modality of time that appears as timelessness. Chapter 3, "An American in Moscow" charts a beginning of Armand Hammer's business in the Soviet Union and his encounter with Lenin as a case in point of exchange relations between market, gift, and state temporalities. In chapter 4, "Time for the field diary," I turn to the temporalities of my own ethnography. I focus on relatedness between research temporality and the temporalities that this research charts. I will be interested in the exchange relationships of state time and research time in the two projects, on a northern Siberian collective and on gifts to Soviet leaders, which provide ethnographic material for this book. The next two chapters constitute this book's conclusion. In these chapters, I ask what are configurations of modernity (Western and Soviet) in specific relations among the various agents and institutions that I chart and that include an American, a Soviet leader, an Evenki hunter, the Kremlin, a Siberian state farm, a Soviet American Concession, and more. I discuss this in chapter 5, "Hobbes' gift," and chapter 6, "Modernity as time."

CHAPTER 2

Lenin and the combined fodder

Vladimir, an Evenki hunter in his 60s (during my fieldwork of 1993–95), was nicknamed "Lenin" for many reasons. First, his first name was the same as the early twentieth-century Soviet leader's name. He visited Moscow and Lenin's Tomb in 1967 and afterward was noted as exhibiting a characteristic hand gesture that reminded people of Lenin. Finally, "Lenin's" wife was named Nadezhda, which echoed the name of the "real" Lenin's wife, Nadezhda Krupskaia. Vladimir is Evenki (pl. *Evenkil*, *ilel*, or *orichil*: "people" or "reindeer people"), a name that identifies a group of Tungus-speaking Subarctic forest (*taiga*) hunters and reindeer herders.

In October 1994, Vladimir came to Katonga village[1] from of his forest reindeer camp, about 50 km north of this settlement. Katonga is the center of a state collective farm on a northern tributary of the Yenisei River, central Siberia. One day, as we were walking to the village store past the collective farm office, the farm director opened his office window (*fortochka*) and yelled at Vladimir: "Come up here at once! Or should I go hunt you down in the forest?" Vladimir walked into the office and found himself shouted at again. As he explained to me, in front of the director, "you always feel guilty of something." But when he managed to inquire what was wrong, the director asked about the combined

---

1. Katonga is a pseudonym for the village where I conducted the fieldwork upon which this and other chapters are based.

fodder. *The* combined fodder. He referred here to an episode that had happened the previous winter and had become a long-standing joke in Katonga throughout 1994.

Combined fodder (*kombikorm*) is an industrially produced fodder for cattle that was widely used in Soviet-era collective farms. The director, named Igor, but referred to by everyone either as the "director" or by his patronymic "Gennadievich," was a Russian man in his mid-50s, who had spent most of his career managing northern state farms. He took pride in the fact that during the hard times of the market transition, he was still able to get fodder for "his" collective. The previous winter, Igor spent quite a lot of time procuring it. He managed somehow to "beat out" (*vybit'*) a subsidy for it in the provincial capital, Krasnoyarsk, purchase the fodder, and truck it to Katonga over the winter road—a long route from the south of the province, which is the only ground access to the area and is cut through the snow every winter only to melt and disappear each spring.

Vladimir was eligible for a few sacks of this fodder for his small reindeer herd and, like other forest Evenki, he was waiting for the collective farm's cross-country vehicle to deliver the fodder to the forest. The cross-country vehicle would normally go around to Evenki forest camps to drop the supplies. This was contingent, however, on the director's success in "beating out" fuel for the vehicle. While the director was away beating the fuel out, herders and hunters were waiting and fueling themselves with spirits. Most had already spent all the money they made from the previous fur-hunting season, and Vladimir sold his portion of the fodder to a Russian villager who could use it to feed pigs.

I heard this story from many sources, most of whom disagreed only about who was the first to start the trade. Whoever this first person was, this act of trade triggered a chain reaction of drinking parties in Katonga. When the director returned with the fuel, he found the entire annual supply of fodder gone, as well as the hunters and herders, who had fled the village guiltily. He launched an investigation in which Vladimir was a plausible candidate for being a culprit in initiating the partying that made the supply of the fodder disappear. But the director also knew his investigation was largely pointless. He needed to be seen to be doing something but was unlikely to get to the bottom of what happened. Commenting to me on this case, as well as on the two decades during which he was in management of northern collectives, Igor said, "The problem is that the state collective farms work fine if you are there managing it. You cannot leave it, and go away for work or on holiday. Once you go away, all falls apart. This is like the *zimniki* [winter roads]." He meant the winter roads that connect these collectives to the mainland.

Developmental time (1): Routes in the forest

This episode reveals multiple temporalities of movement of forest Evenki, collective farm administrators, and material objects such as the fodder. In this chapter, I use this episode as a crossing point between linear time of development, cyclical temporalities of infrastructure and travel, and a time that appears to be outside time, that is, timelessness. In the sections that follow, I introduce these temporalities and discuss relations between them. The point of this discussion is to highlight relations of *change* between them (see chapter 1).

Combined fodder was a standard part of collective farm economy. But in this area the fodder and this very collective economy was also "help," ubiquitous in the Soviet state discourse on "development of indigenous peoples of the north" (*razvitie korennyh narodov Severa*). This development was to bridge a spatial isolation of Siberian north and the temporal or evolutionary distance between indigenous and Soviet ways of life. It consisted in a maximum possible approximation of life in the north to that of rural collective farms in central Russia and, ideally, the Soviet industrial society.

In this particular area, nomadic hunting-gathering and reindeer herding of Evenki were the targets of this development. The Soviet collectivization of the 1930s, and the construction of institutions such as local soviets took place there as elsewhere in the Soviet Union, but with a distinct developmental connotation. It was accompanied with boarding-school education, set for the children of nomadic hunters and herders, and with attempts to settle these nomads down in purposefully enlarged villages in the 1960–70s. I conducted fieldwork in Katonga in 1988–89 and 1993–95, when many Evenki combined village jobs with forest hunting but some, like Vladimir and Nadezhda, stayed in the forest most of the year and only occasionally came out to the village.

In this subarctic area, "development" as a version of the time of progress was embedded in a chronotope of "forest" versus "village" lifestyles and identities as well as in the seasonal temporalities of infrastructure of travel and access. This area is part of the northern permafrost zone. Katonga is located on the banks of the Podkamennaia Tunguska, which is Russian for the "Stony River of the Tungus." The Tungus is the Russian colonial name for the Evenki. The designation of the tributary of the Yenisei as "stony" follows from rapids that separate the upper part of this river from the rest of the Yenisei basin and make it inaccessible by riverboat most of the year, apart from the short period of spring flood.

The only ground access to the village is by seasonal winter routes. Otherwise, the village gets supplies by boat once a year, at the time of spring flood, when cargo boats can sail up to Katonga over the rapids. There are flights to the village from the regional center Baikit by a small Antonov biplane that lands in winter on river ice and in summer on a tiny airstrip in a glade cleared from the forest, about three kilometers from the village. In Soviet times, these flights came in twice a week, except for the late spring and early autumn, when ice was melting on the river and the unpaved airstrip turned into a swamp of either melting snow or autumn rain. After the collapse of the Soviet Union, state subsidies for these flights were also gone, and the flights became much less frequent and the tickets became more expensive. There were helicopter flights, also from the regional center, which could land right in the middle of the village, no matter how solid or soggy the ground was. But they were even more expensive as they consumed more fuel, and thus were even less frequent.

The trucks that used winter routes were the cheapest, in terms of the ratio of cargo they could bring to the fuel they spent. These routes are not paved roads but ground roads that run through the forest from the south. Trucks pave these routes in early winter when the moss that covers permafrost freezes and can therefore take the weight of the truck. Once this road is paved in snow, traffic to northern villages is frequent enough to not be stopped by snowfalls. By December, such routes are solid tracks coming over the snow, rammed with each passing of a truck. But these routes melt every spring, and they have to be built anew every year.

Developmental time (ii): Paths to noncapitalism

Here, developmental time is simultaneously a frame of a long-term time of progress and a frame of cyclical rhythms of infrastructure of access. Deliveries of combined fodder, not just to the village but also to reindeer herds in the forest, were part of the plan to bring a greater regularity to forest nomadism that was to achieve the same purpose. Another component of the package of this "help" was a project to build reindeer fences to fix territories where reindeer migrate seasonally, and in doing so make herding easier. I started my first fieldwork in this region in 1988 by working in a brigade that was to construct such fences in a neighboring collective farm. "When we have the area fenced in," the director

of that farm explained to me, "they [Evenki] won't hav
the time and move camps along the reindeer migratioɪ
kochevaniia]; then we can deliver combined fodder to tl
permanent bases in the center of the fenced areas—say, fɩ
pasture. There will be a proper [wooden] house, a sauna,
small school for kids." In this instance of what James Scoɪ
as "seeing like a state," reindeer moved in an orderly and leꜱ ꜱ fashion from
one fenced area to another, where they consume lichen and, at assigned places,
the combined fodder; Evenki orderly moved from one seasonal residence to
another; and children grew up studying near their relatives—and not in village
boarding school—and learn reindeer herding in addition to standard school
subjects.

The particular designs of orderly reindeer herding were short-lived as they
were created in the late 1970s and 1980s and were brought to an end by the collapse of the Soviet Union. But these designs have a complex archaeology back
in Soviet history. They were preceded by collective farm enlargement and indigenous sedentarization as a "solution" of the problem of nomadism (1960–70s),
and before that, by collectivization of the 1930s, "adapted" to the "special conditions" of the north—namely, by what Soviet reformers and ethnographers
understood as a combination of precapitalist hunting-gathering and reindeer
herding modes of production and colonial capitalism. *Help* was the main idiom
of all these reforms, and continuously so since the establishment, during the late
1920s, of "culture bases" [*kul'tbasy*] that were to start Soviet reforms and become
centers of Soviet culture, education, and hygiene, as well as depositories of ethnographic knowledge, et cetera. This was preceded by *help* as in hunger relief in
the aftermath of the Civil War in the early 1920s. For Scott, such schemes to
improve human condition by making social life legible and predictable inevita-
bly fail; in my perspective, what is interesting about such projects is how they are
capable of rising from the ashes. All these developmental projects did not work
according to their design; there is a temporal cyclicality of projects, in addition
to the linearity of their concepts of time, as their respective forms of "help" that
were coming around as new forms of order and new solutions to the problems
of chronic failure (Ssorin-Chaikov 2016).

The ideology of this help was linear and explicitly linked with Lenin-the-
Soviet-leader's views on noncapitalist development. These views permeate his
writings from the 1899 treatise *The development of capitalism in Russia* onward
(Lenin 1971). But most explicitly, they were formulated after the Revolution of

in the speech that Lenin gave for the Commission on the National and Colonial Question of the II Congress of the Comintern (July 26, 1920):

> The question that was put forward to us was the following: can we consider as correct the thesis that the capitalist stage of development of peoples' economy [*narodnogo khozaistva*] is inevitable for those backward peoples that are now liberating themselves, and among which now, after the [First World] War, progress is visible. We have answered this question in the negative. If the revolutionary, victorious proletariat carries out systematic propaganda work among them, and if soviet governments come *helping* with all the means in their disposal, then it is incorrect to believe that the capitalist stage is inevitable for the backward peoples. In all colonies and backward countries we need not merely to form independent cadres of fighters [for communism], that is, party organizations, not only to conduct propaganda for the organization of peasant soviets, and strive to adapt them to the pre-capitalist conditions, but the Communist International [itself] needs to establish and justify theoretically the thesis that with the *help* of the proletariat of the advanced countries the backward countries can come to the soviet order bypassing certain states of development—[come] to communism bypassing the capitalist stage. (Lenin 1981: 245–46; emphasis added)

Note a clear linear temporal vision of this view. Countries and peoples are divided into categories of "advanced" and "backward." The colonized are considered as politically contiguous with the exploited working classes in the "advanced" countries. Lenin argued that former Czarist "colonies" such as Turkestan, Central Asia, show a similar "backward" condition and valuable experience of Bolshevik work (Lenin 1981: 244). Elsewhere, he stated that this path of non-capitalist development is applicable to Mongolia, as the first foreign country that follows Soviet Russia in communist reforms (Lenin 1970a: 233). In turn, Soviet ethnographers and reformers elaborated these views for various regions of the Soviet Union. The magisterial *Noncapitalist path of development of the small peoples of the north* by Mikhail Sergeev (1955) remains one of the most detailed theoretical elaborations and historical surveys of Soviet reforms from this point of view.

Here, linear time is installed by the gift of development ("help"), had both class and postcolonial connotations, and has visible analogies with developmental time elsewhere. What makes the Soviet case distinct is a historical longevity of this idiom of developmental time that stems not from "the Marshall plan for the Third World" (Escobar 1995; Cooper and Packard 1997) but from the constitution of the Second World out of Marxist revolutionary time (Hanson 1997). The temporality of the revolutionary leap forward that I introduced with the example of the gift to Lenin of the figurine, *Eritis sicut deus* (see chapter 1; see also fig. 1, p. xiv), overlaps with the temporality of assistance and paternalism toward "backward peoples" of noncapitalist periphery of a self-identified post-capitalism of the Soviet project. If Lenin himself "ate" from the tree of knowledge, daring to be "as gods" (see chapter 1), the parents and grandparents of the Evenki "Lenin" were a part of a multitude of "the people" from the former Russian empire who received what followed from this Lenin's knowledge: the gifts of noncapitalism. Evenki "Lenin" himself was taken by the romance of developmental expectations in the 1960s when he began his career and was as a Young Communist (*Komsomol*) activist (I detail this further in chapter 4).

To a large extent, he remained a "conscript of modernity" (D. Scott 2004) in the 1990s, as was Igor, the Katonga collective farm director, who thought about his own career in terms of a genuine "civilizing mission." This was despite the fact that Soviet developmental order in the 1990s was in ruins, and despite the fact that the director's own education and work took place during late socialism when these Marxist idioms were taken with cynicism and pragmatism (Yurchak 2006). Yet, as I argue elsewhere (Ssorin-Chaikov 2016), for his generation of Siberian bureaucracy, the teleological temporality of Lenin's noncapitalist development was transformed into the "depoliticized" (Ferguson 1994)—that is, simply "true" temporality of "civilization as such," "simply civilization," or "normal civilization" (*normal'naia tsivilizatsia*). This is one of the instances of change relations between temporalities. The time of development was thought to be Marxist, but it turns out to be "simply civilization" (X is in fact Y: see chapter 1). As one regional bureaucrat told me in 1995, "This is amazing [*porazitepl'no*]: many Evenki still huddle in their *chumy* [conic tents]. We need to do something to help." Igor, too, thought of this *tsivilizatsia* as a gift. He was angry about the waste of the combined fodder, but in this anger there is also a disappointment that the recipients of this gift are ungrateful: "you see, Nikolai, they just don't seem to care about what we give to them."

Disruptions (i): October

To sum up: the long-term linear developmental time can be seen as "consisting" in shorter and cyclical intervals of seasonal temporalities of infrastructure, and the couple of decades-long temporalities of developmental projects, but also of their transformations. Seasonal deliveries of the combined fodder, or seasonal travel of children to boarding schools, were supposed to add up to progress eventually. I will argue now that these cyclical temporalities also had a capacity to disrupt and in fact modify the linearity of developmental time.

In the fall of 1994, I made several trips from the forest to Katonga, accompanying different people who were going back and forth. That fall—like many falls—was a season when various links between the forest Evenki and the village overlap and intensify. Forest children are brought over to start their school year. Forest Evenki buy supplies for the upcoming hunting season. The acts of both taking children to school and trade are recurrent seasonal activities. But throughout the 1990s they were put under new pressures from the postsocialist market economy. The state no longer provided helicopters to collect children from forest camps. Trade had become private and the inflation that had several times diminished the value of monetary incomes had now the effect of revitalizing barter. There were conflicts over exchange in which the market both disrupted and reinforced links between the forest and the village (Ssorin-Chaikov 2000). There were negotiations and frictions with the school over the timing of children's arrival and their very availability for state education. Teachers ask, "Have they all come? Why some are late for the beginning of school year?"

But these frictions were also cyclical and they have, in fact, predated the collapse of the Soviet Union. Even before this time, the children would often "miss" the helicopter and join their parents in October for their village trade trip. In turn, the parents were needed in the village for the fall collective farm meetings. But there was always a point of uncertainty about the timing of Evenki arrival in the village. While these visits are regular, seasonal activities, in no way do they have fixed itineraries—even if they are linked to a fixed arrival date, for example, to the beginning of the school year on September 1. Departure is decided on the day itself by the head of a family tent or a camp that travels. It can catch by surprise all who are interested in going. Hunters who may happen to be away that day risk missing the boat. At the end of September and early October that year, I waited for Vladimir to decide for a couple of weeks and in the end went to Katonga with another party. Departure to the village is not as sudden as, for example, hunters' decisions for hunting, when you might wake up and see their beds empty. But it follows the same logic of reluctance to speak about the future. It is *ngolymo gune diuloshki*, Evenki for "forbidden to speak about what is ahead." This "speaking," that is, telling that we plan to leave tomorrow, makes you visible for spirits (*buhadyl* and *hargil*) that may harm your fortune. But if hunting is an individual activity, not telling exactly when we leave for the village creates a temporary collective hierarchy between those who decide (e.g., Vladimir) and those who wait for the decision.

Disruptions (ii): Combined fodder

There is a growing body of work that discusses temporalities of Tungus nomadism (Lavrillier 2005; Ssorin-Chaikov 2003; Safonova and Sántha 2013; Brandisauskas 2016; Ulturgasheva 2012). But the combined fodder episode, with which I started this chapter, reveals the rhythms of nomadism of both forest Evenki and collective farm directors. Let me conceptualize it as a single rhythm.

The temporality of their movement and infrastructure partially mirror each other. The easiest and the fastest way for Evenki to come to the village was by reindeer sleigh in winter, and the sleigh route was similarly beaten through the snow at the time when trucks have taken the farm director away from the village and brought back the combined fodder and other cargo. Just as with truck routes, this sleigh traffic ground to a halt when snow started to melt in late April. When small forest rivers flood, movement stops not just between the forest and the village but also between forest camps, as these small and quiet rivers turn large and rough. But just as the cyclicality of Evenki forest nomadism could be and in fact was disruptive of the cyclicality of the developmental time, so was the cyclicality of the fodder deliveries and of the collective farm order.

Let me come back to Igor's comment: "The problem is that the state collectives work fine if you are there managing it. You cannot leave it, and go away for work or on holiday. Once you go away, all falls apart. This is like the *zimniki* [winter roads]." This comparison speaks volumes both about the temporality of infrastructure in the north and about a continuous physical effort that apparently needed to be applied to run it, beat it, ram it—and all that only to be repeated all over the next winter. The Russian word for "beating through" (*probit'*)—as in "to beat the road through the snow"—shares the verbal root "to beat" (*bit'*) or "to beat out" (*vybit'*)—as in "beating out the resources" such as the combined fodder or the fuel for the cross-country vehicle, although this "beating" is out of the state, and not through the snow. This physicality of effort had a particular temporality. Just as in the matter of the winter road, a successful provision of resources once does not mean that their seamless flow is to follow. The effort must be repeated each time.

"We wanted to do better, but it turned out as always"

If combined fodder as help inaugurates the linear time of progress, another temporality makes an appearance in cyclical difficulties in getting it to Katonga. The director was talking to me about backwardness, about failure to move up the ladder of development—in other words, about the location of Evenki in the linear order of time. But it was also about much more than backwardness: about things sliding into chaos, which is not only historically stable but furthermore incorrigible. This was not merely sliding back in time but into another time altogether. He could not know a phrase that the Russian prime minister of that time, Victor Chernomyrdin, was yet to coin: "We wanted to do better, but it turned out as always," but he meant something similar. When he made reference to winter routes that melt every spring, I thought about how Hobbesian was this order, which needed to be maintained by the act of will, which must be constantly renewed. The act of will constituted a linear temporal vector but the Leviathan did not seem to be able to take permanent root. It was the state of nature that appeared to be a temporal invariable, something permanent, if constantly bubbling under such matters of director's concern such as the combined fodder and the timing of arrival of the forest hunters and herders in the village.

The Soviet developmental view of time had, of course, included its own concept of eternity. But this was the eternity of the end (communism) that cast its shadow across all preceding time. Katherine Verdery (1996) alludes to this quality of time that, for the Communist Party, was "culminating" to the point "of becoming *for all time*," brilliantly captured by a Romanian joke: "What . . . [did] we celebrate on 8 May 1821 [May 8, 1921 being the Communist Party foundation date]? One hundred years until the founding of the Romanian Communist Party" (1996: 57). But the point of this joke is echoed by not-at-all-joking Henri Barbusse in his Stalin panegyric, where Stalin's figure "is raised full-length" not just over Europe and Asia but also "over the past and the future" (Barbusse 1935: 2). Boris Groys remarks of Soviet art that the socialist revolution's claim to have sped up historical time in fact froze it: "The avant-garde and the subsequent Stalinist art is driven by a utopian desire to stop time, to find themselves on the other side of history . . . outside historical time in the 'time-space' of the Golden Age" (2003: 118–19). In turn, Alexei Yurchak (2006) has argued that the late Soviet order had a distinct temporality of being "forever," independent of its teleological end.

But this Siberian "state of nature," a permanent chaos into which things "always" slide, is a different kind of *always*, and it makes up a different kind of *forever*. To me, it has analogies with earlier imaginations of the temporality of Siberian colonial order. Consider the remarks of a mid-nineteenth-century Russian Orthodox commentator Nil, the Archbishop of Irkutsk. In his Siberian memoirs, he notes the impressive progress made by the Orthodox faith among the Tungus, who "like Mongolians . . . started to accept Baptism" in the early eighteenth century. However, this progress could not be taken for granted, and missions needed constant maintenance because "nobody can guarantee that baptized parents have baptized children." Once missionary activities stopped or simply slowed down, the Tungus, "in their wandering and dispersed ways, were lost from sight and sank, so to speak, into the sea of forests." The metaphor of the sea appears in Nil's account as he cites Scripture in wondering if Siberian forests were not dissimilar to the primordial emptiness of the world before the Creation: "Wasn't that the way our planet just emerged from the primeval ocean, and wasn't it simply empty and void?" And then he puts this in the words of Ovid:

> In that entire world, Nature had one appearance—
> Of matter, rude and irregular,
> Of ever changing, unrelated, discordant substances. (Nil 1874: 120–21, 194)

The linear time of missionary conversion here is contrasted with "matter, rude and irregular." In Ovid, and in Christianity, the place of this chaos is in a linear temporal order. "Ever changing, unrelated, discordant substances" are those of the world before Creation. Unlike the Leviathan of Christianity or Soviet development, this "primeval ocean" always has a potential to expand without constant maintenance work. Both the collective farm director and Archbishop Nil "discover" the temporality of the state of nature in the liner time of development and Christian conversion. Underneath these linear vectors they see something else: a historically stable chaos, which tends to structurally repeat itself.

Change between temporalities

The combined fodder episode then can be seen as a material example of a "transtemporal hinge" (Pedersen and Nielsen 2013) where it works as a window into two different temporal ontologies. What makes it different from a "hinge," however, is that the two temporalities are not equal in terms of their potentialities, narratives of the past, and their configurations of the present.

In Igor's eyes, developmental time, and the state of affairs in which things are forever like winter roads that melt every spring, are statements of truth. It is not a matter of what is preferable (see, for example, Pedersen and Nielsen 2013: 127–29) but of what actually happens. The regime of truth makes this discovery of chaos an instance of change, which I introduced in chapter 1 as a mode of relations between different temporalities. Temporality of the world was thought to be X, but is *in fact* not X but Y, with "X" being linear developmental time and "Y" being the timelessness of the "state of nature." The relation "X is in fact Y" (X equals Y, X = Y) works only one way: X trumps Y. Y is Y, but Y is not X. Discovery here is a linear movement from one temporality to another. It takes place on the grounds of the truth-value of each of these frameworks, and to maintain one of them is possible only at the expense of the other.

Furthermore, this inequality of time X and time Y is itself a mode of relatedness. The transformation from one to another is not instant. The "hinge" between X and Y, and a passage from one to another is itself an event or a series of events that entails its own temporality and its own relatedness. Let us come back to my conversations with the collective farm director in the aftermath of his encounter with Vladimir "Lenin." This conversation happened in October; the combined fodder episode took place the previous March. The director did not have a chance to see Vladimir since the episode, and the argument took place as a part of the director's sporadically run investigation into this waste. It was sporadic as it depended on forest hunters and herders being in the village, which they visited only a few times a year following the cycles of ecological, trade, and administrative temporalities. It was also sporadic as the director, the sole investigator in this inquiry, was away a lot, including for portions of that October (Ssorin-Chaikov 2000). Plus, Igor had to remember to address this issue on meeting the hunters and herders. This depended on his mood, which in turn depended on other "wrongs," which in his view the collective farmers were guilty of at a given moment.

That October, I was in Katonga for a few days, staying with village relatives of the Evenki whom I knew in the forest, and researching this period of intense and contentious sociality, while also trying to navigate my way to avoid the excessive partying that accompanied such village visits. I ended up spending quite a lot of time in the director's house—he kindly offered me the chance to rest there and to enjoy his extensive collection of films. Katonga did not have a television antenna to receive and transmit the TV signal locally, and although many people had television sets, they were used mostly for watching films on tapes that were brought from the regional center, Baikit, or from Krasnoyarsk, by whoever was able to travel there during these difficult times.

The day after the row between Vladimir and Igor, I spent a few hours at Igor's home, watching these movies and reading while the director and his wife were at work. The director returned home rather early, at about 4 p.m. He asked if I wanted to join him for a shot of vodka and an early supper. I declined the drink but joined him for the meal. We set down at the kitchen table. He was still bursting with anger about the combined fodder. I did not have to ask him to turn the conversation this way. I told him that Vladimir did not deny that he was one of the first to sell his share, but claimed that he only sold his portion to get hunting supplies, that he "did not know anything about the drunks," and left Katonga immediately after getting his supplies. "A likely story," remarked the director. All suspects apparently gave similar stories.

There is no paper trail of his investigation, but the situation is reminiscent of colonial inquiries described by Ann Stoler. They lock the stable after the horses have already bolted. "When nothing else works and no decision can be reached, 'appoint a commission' was a favorite response of colonial authorities," she quotes in a study of Dutch Java (Stoler 2010: 30). Her point is, however, broader. Commissions of inquiry are not merely signs of the imperial entropy but of productive forces of their own. Information they collect and identity judgments they make shape colonial situations. I take this insight further by noting that the investigation is also a temporality. In the case of the combined fodder episode, the linearity of developmental time that brought the fodder to collective farms and "civilization" to Siberian reindeer herders is replicated in the linearity of investigative time in which the director looked for the person who started the trade. If it was possible, even purely theoretically, to get to the truth about this first person, then the Katonga collective could be classed into more or less guilty persons—distinguishing the ones who initiated the trade from others who followed and those who did not participate and were therefore not guilty at all. This classifying order mirrors the linear organization of development. There are leaders and followers, initiators and respondents. This is a development that was led astray. This line of flight had its own linearity, with the combined fodder incident making it a waste rather than a progress. But this could be reversed if the culprits were identified. One or several guilty persons are impediments to development, but they do not undermine development and its linear time of progress as a mode of social organization.

However, the point is that it was not merely difficult but, for all sorts of practical reasons, quite impossible for the director to identify guilty instigators. Furthermore, he told me that in a way he knew that from the start. This linear temporality of the investigation was not quite linear. It was simultaneously one that was moody, punctuated (the investigation was sporadic rather than constant), and bordering its own chaos. Furthermore, the time of investigation was in the end wasted in addition to the fodder, as the investigation was not merely impossible but pointless (*bezsmyslennoe*, "without sense"). The whole collective was guilty of wasting the combined fodder and, at the same time, not guilty at all because it was incorrigible. "All are guilty, but what can you take from them" (*da vse oni vinovaty, no chto s nikh vziat'*), as Igor put it. "What do you except," said he specifically about Vladimir "Lenin," adding a Russian saying, "a wolf looks back the forest no matter how long it is fed [*skol' volka ne kormi, on vse v les gliadit*]." For the director, it was this that in fact transpired in the linear time of the investigation. It seems that it is not only the investigative time that was wasted here but also developmental time as well. Yet this waste of time is no waste as a signification of the state of nature. Failed investigation, paradoxically, succeeded in doing this. It *made* an undifferentiated mass of "children of nature" by failing to produce an atomized distribution of the collective into a multitude of the initiators and the followers that mirrors the linear distribution of stages in the time of development.

A Russian phrase "to wave the hand" (*makhnut' rukoi*) is close to "waiving"—it means to give up doing something. When the director thought, "they just don't seem to care about what we give to them," he "waved the hand," and gave up. He gave up his investigation, and at that point gave up development. During a meal in his kitchen, he said, "I don't care then too" (*mne togda tozhe vse ravno*); this was after he came back from work at about 4 p.m. During that day he spent some time radio-calling forest camps. Then he worked on the collective farm bookkeeping and had a few conversations with his deputy for hunting. At that point he "did not care," not only if the combined fodder was wasted but also if reindeer were lost, as they apparently were that week in one of the forest brigades. He also did not care if preparation for hunting did not go in the orderly fashion. He "waved the hand" giving it up to the already existing semiprivate relations between Evenki fur hunters and semilegal fur traders (Ssorin-Chaikov 2000). When he had his conversation with Vladimir the day before, he gave in to a sudden request by Vladimir to "privatize" Vladimir's small reindeer herd—that is, to take it out of one of the reindeer brigades and come out of the system of state collective farm employment.

"Giving up" (as in "waving the hand") and "giving in" to privatization were to enter into relations in which resources were given out—very much for free and almost as gifts—at that point in time in the early post-Soviet transition state. As far as the gift of development was concerned, the director felt sad, if not offended: "they just don't seem to care about what we *give* to them [my emphasis]." Post-Soviet transition at that time seemed not as gift that someone gave out but as something that was just lying out there for free. These were social relations of "wild" privatization, which here as elsewhere in Russia were often described as "grabitization" (*prikhvatizatsiia*). In these social relations—which exist in the time of this state of nature—everything becomes this *nature* out there, almost like John Locke's America. The difference here is between the land with no work on it done, in Locke's eyes, before colonists arrived on the one hand, and the Soviet case where all previous work on the land was canceled as meaningless, and the land and its spoils became out there "free" for new enclosures, on the other hand.

Limits of change

Johannes Fabian argues that modern time is often conveyed through abbreviation. He grounds this in the Renaissance techniques of memory that are transformed into the instruments of representation—for instance, in the work of Jacques-Beninge Boussuet, a court theologian of Louis XIV. For him, the possibility to see universal history as a "general map" of linear time in relation to "particular map"—that is, histories of individual country and people—relies on representational devices that allow us to see "the order of times" in "the sequence of things, "for instance, in artifacts in Cabinets of Curiosities. These are devices of abbreviation, which make this order apparent at a single glance. But the effectiveness of these devices is contingent on the assumption of universality—the universality of human history—that designates the world in its totality that is visible in all its parts (Fabian 1983: 4).

This is an a priori assumption; it is important for Fabian's argument that it works as such. The totality of the universal history as time is posited prior to definition of any *part*, however it may be defined. As a representation of historical time, this technique is an example of B-series time (see Gell 1992) that is based on a clear distinction of *before* and *after*. This B-series time is the time of an argument of the Enlightenment philosophers of history that, according to Fabian, *first* make this a priori assumption of universal history and *then* class parts of the world, peoples, and artifacts within the scheme that is produced in this way. In terms of B-series as relationships between temporalities, universal history is *before* particular history. In this form, the argument is deductive—that is, it posits the general first and the particular second.

I have already compared Hobbes to the Siberian time of development and time of the state of nature. Indeed, both Russian imperial and Soviet "civilizing missions" in Siberia bear resemblance to the Enlightenment project. Here, too, the switch between the two temporalities works through abbreviation. The change does not happen when the combined fodder is wasted or when "Tungus baptized parents" fail to baptize their children. It happens when the farm director or the Archbishop Nil talk or write about this, or the collective director acts on this by conducting an investigation. The abbreviation does not even have to operate through an articulated narrative, as in the citation from Ovid that sums up Nil's narrative. It could be made visible with a hint, a shaking of shoulders, or a gesture of waving the hand. For Evenki "Lenin," the term *combined fodder* sufficed; for the director, the notion of *winter road* that melts every spring was sufficient. Among (mostly Russian) regional bureaucrats of the Evenki District, a line from Alexander Pushkin's rendition of Horace's *Exegi Monumentum*, "the presently wild Tungus" (*i nyne dikii, tungus*), was sufficient as a means of pointing to the incorrigible state of nature where the Tungus belonged.

The kind of abbreviation that is at work in the Siberian context is organized similarly to the instruments of temporal classification that Fabian describes; at the same, it illustrates a different process. My point is that a translation of one totality (the universal narrative of progress) into another one (the state of nature) appears as a linear, one-way transition. But it is also interesting to note that both visions could be in fact achieved simultaneously. This works by making visible cracks in individual parts of development—such as the fate of the combined fodder or the fate of missionary activity. But the individual parts can either be parts of universal linear temporality (Christian or Soviet) and of the place of Evenki it in, or it could be about the permanent state of nature in which there is no linear time at all. In fact, a means of making one of these two totalities visible is through an equally a priori doubt about which these parts refer to, and what comes first. Shaking shoulders and saying, "what did you expect, these are 'the Tungus, presently wild,'" may equally be a means of discovery of linear time of progress that is desired, and a discovery of the timelessness of the state of nature that actually takes place. Also, it is difficult to ascertain the temporal and causal sequence between a crack in the system—say, of the ill fate of the combined fodder—and the system, that is, a particular temporality. Both totalities of linear time and timelessness are a priori assumptions that are out of the time they describe. If so, does it really not matter what is the cause and what is the effect here? Do cracks have to be there *first* for this doubt in progress to appear and transition to timelessness of chaos to be discovered? These transformations of temporalities are not quite inductive. The doubt may and often does precede cracks; this makes them not only *after* the doubt but also, in fact, almost unnecessary. It is the doubt itself that signifies, and not the proof that follows. The director and the regional bureaucrats had disappointment and sadness with regard to the gift of development. Yet their comments also contained a certainty. They sort of knew it before it happened: "Of course they wasted it," "Of course everybody got drunk," "Of course it is impossible to say who started it." This *of course* means that the doubt is already there, and that it is not really a doubt but a deep conviction about who the collective farmers really are.

And it is important to keep in mind that this deep conviction is simultaneously revealed in the statements that, first, "this is amazing how many Evenki still huddle in their *chumy* [conic tents]" and therefore "we need to do something to help," and, second, that "we wanted to do better but it turned out as always." The cracks are the same but they are reassembled differently. If so, the discovery (change) between temporalities is akin to a turn of a kaleidoscope that recombines a pattern of parts as an entirely different yet entirely coherent whole. In other words, the relationships I discuss here are ultimately reversible. It is not simply a matter of the state of nature being true while the linear time of development or Christian conversion is not. If anything, the state of nature invites Leviathan back. It is a necessary foundation for keeping development or missionary practices in place. In other words, it is not merely that the state of nature is "discovered"; so is the Leviathan.

Let me give an example. My conversation with members of regional administration about the combined fodder episode happened after my conversations with the collective farm director. They did respond first in a manner similar to the director's; namely, that the development is pointless. "What do you expect?" said one of them off the record. We were standing on the porch of the administration building after a formal interview ended; it was early spring, 1995. "Where are you now?" he then asked. "I am coming back to Katonga, to the forest [*v taigu*]." He again replied with the now-familiar phrase, quoted above: "This is amazing how many Evenki still huddle in their *chumy* [conic tents]. We need to do something to help."

This conversation illustrates how, on the one hand, the failure to manufacture modernity works as a means of discovery of the incorrigible state of nature. On the other hand, this is also a rediscovery of a necessity of development. Let us look closer at this simultaneity. The two frameworks are there together but in conversations and in social relations not quite at the same time. There is certainty—"of course, they wasted it," "what do you expect?"—that at one moment leads to a narrative transition to the state of nature. Here, the corresponding social relation is what unites the two of us, an anthropologist and a regional administrator *as if* sharing blank truth about indigenous Siberia, that "we wanted to do better but it turned out as always" (although this is a shared opinion only from the point of view of the bureaucrat). At this particular point of time, "help" is pointless (as it was the day the director finished work at 4 p.m., came home, and we talked). But when the conversation turns to my travel to this so-called state of nature, what comes forward is the idiom of such travel. From the point of view of this regional bureaucrat and his inspections (of which he did many, particularly counting state reindeer), and from the point of view of Soviet and Russian ethnographic travel, this is the state traveling to the wilderness with the purpose of delivering help, development, and the ethnographic description of what was there *before*. At this point in time, the kaleidoscope turns and the pattern of the incorrigible state of nature is reassembled as the linear time of development and state ethnography. Our social relations now, literally in the next sentence of our conversation, were to become those of purposeful fellow state travelers, in which it did not matter that at that point I was coming to Katonga from Stanford University and he was coming from Russian regional administration.

Both temporalities have a temporary appearance, which orders the collective farm of combined fodder and people in a particular assemblage. The state of nature suddenly flashes and next, in a particular rhythm, the figure of the bureaucrat as an embodiment of the time of development materializes equally suddenly, like Koroviev in Bulgakov's *Master and Margarita*. This happens when Vladimir "Lenin" entertained the possibility of quitting the collective farm but opted instead to stay within it, or when the director felt it to be necessary to appear to be doing something about the waste of the fodder. The Archbishop Nil's "matter, rude and irregular" and the order trade places. In the first instance, the state of nature is discovered in the failures of development; in the second instance, development is reinstituted. In other words, what we see here is a substitution, or an operation of exchange. The exchange happens between temporal frameworks that structure the notions of permanent chaos and linear development. But substitutions happen within these frameworks, too. The linear time of Christian missions in Siberia is not the same as the linear time of socialist modernization. In each of these notions of linear time, the state of nature is also different. Exchange between them is also their *change*. At this point, let me turn to my example of Armand Hammer's gift to Vladimir Lenin-the-Soviet-Leader.

CHAPTER 3

An American in Moscow

In the summer of 1921, Armand Hammer (1898–1990), later a powerful business magnate who ran Occidental Petroleum in 1957–90 and founded the Armand Hammer Museum of Art, Los Angeles, was a 23-year-old graduate of Columbia Medical School, waiting to start his residency at Bellevue Hospital in New York. He was to wait six months between his graduation in June and the beginning of his residency in January 1922. While he waited, he responded to what he took to be a pressing matter, one that was unfolding overseas. In Russia's Volga river region, an eight-week-long severe drought had "fields burned barren" (Hammer and Lyndon 1987: 88), which destroyed the future harvest and forced hundreds of thousands of peasants to besiege Volga cities where, in addition to hunger, an epidemic of typhus broke out. Hammer, who had been combining his medical studies with work for his family company, Allied Drugs, decided to join in an international humanitarian effort to alleviate the famine. He brought $60,000 worth of surgical equipment and pharmaceutical chemicals to Soviet Russia in hopes of donating them to set up a field hospital in the hunger-stricken region. When he arrived in Moscow, however, he had to wait again—first, for his equipment to arrive from Riga where it was delayed by customs, and second, for the Soviet Commissariat of Health to receive him and grant permission to work in a field hospital.

He spent his time between the Commissariat for Foreign Affairs where he needed to register his passport, and the Commissariat for Health where he made his donation, which was gratefully received, but where he discovered that a relevant official who could authorize his field hospital plan was apparently away for about a month. Time was running short. Hammer was frustrated by this delay (almost to the point of abandoning the idea altogether and returning to the United States), but was then invited to spend a month on a train trip to the Urals. The trip was organized for a group of foreign visitors to assess the situation in this industrial area, which was also affected by famine. He jumped at the opportunity, but had to wait again for another three days; he showed up at the railway station every night only to learn that the departure had been "postponed till tomorrow" (Hammer and Lyndon 1987: 106). On the fourth day, he telephoned the station and received a firm confirmation that train would leave that night at 5 p.m. But when he went there, there was no one who knew when the train was to leave or from where. He eventually found his way by following other passengers—whom he heard speaking English—to a platform where a train finally departed at 11 p.m.

The train slowly pushed through the hunger-ridden terrain of the Volga area toward Ekaterinburg and still farther east. The full effects of the drought were to be felt later in autumn, when food from the previous season would really be spent, with no grain harvest to replace it. When the train halted for a few hours at a whistle-stop east of Ekaterinburg, Hammer and other passengers went for walk toward a nearby village and passed a small hut where an old man was making a coffin for himself. "I am all alone, you understand, and I have food for three more weeks only, and then I must die. But before that I will have made my coffin and will lie in it to await death so that I shall not be buried like a dog in the bare ground" (Hammer and Lyndon 1987: 111). It was striking for Hammer that this was happening in the Urals, where "lay the greatest treasures of the world—the richest mines of platinum, emeralds, asbestos, copper and almost every known mineral—yet the people were unable to utilize them even to provide themselves with the barest necessities of life and were starving to death" (Hammer and Lyndon 1987: 111). In fact, he found out that storages in Ekaterinburg and other places were full of these riches. He asked why these valuables were not exported in order to purchase grain. The reply was that this would be useless. The European blockade had just been lifted and it would take too long to sell these valuables to do anything for the starving people.

It was then that he was struck with a thought. "I can arrange it for you," he said to his Soviet hosts, suggesting that he could accomplish this quickly via his company in New York, Allied Drugs. "Is there anyone around here with authority to make a contract?" (Hammer and Lyndon 1987: 109). The Ekaterinburg Soviet meeting was called. Hammer was told that one million bushels of wheat were needed as a minimum to alleviate hunger. He knew that in the United States that year there was a very good harvest, and wheat was traded for a dollar per bushel. But once the price went below a dollar, farmers preferred to burn wheat rather than sell it. Hammer told the Ekaterinburg Soviet that he could use a million dollars to purchase a million bushels of wheat on credit and ship it to Russia on the condition that in return, every ship would take the Ural valuables. He immediately telegraphed Allied Drugs to get the deal going. The deal included a 5 percent commission for Hammer for each of the two parts of it—for the purchase of grain and sale of valuables. He stresses in his memoirs, however, that at that time he was only thinking about hunger relief and not at all about profit, but he needed the commission to reassure his American partners that he was serious and that they could send grain to Russia without fear of financial loss, and in doing so "help the Russians to save the Ural population from starving" (Hammer and Lyndon 1987: 109).

Given time

Hammer's trip was entangled in the combined temporality of urgency and delays. The trip took time, and more than Hammer expected. But Hammer used this time. He capitalized on the crisis that he saw as well as on the waiting time that he had to spend—from waiting for a hospital residency in New York to delays in the bureaucratic time of the early Soviet state to the slowness of time that characterized the emerging Soviet foreign trade. It is the latter's slow time that Hammer offered to speed up. And his decision seems to have come just as quickly as it did when he seized the opportunity to take the trip from the United States to Russia, and from Moscow to the Urals.

But this trip's crucial episode, the deal to swap grain for the Ural valuables, did not just *take* time, however instant; it also *gave* time: Hammer offered to speed up the time that it would take to set up the trade, which would be loo long to do the job—that is, to alleviate hunger. But this given time—the offer to speed the time of hunger relief—is quite complex. First, the time that Hammer *gave* by speeding up this process is time he was able to *take*—that is, the credit that Hammer was able to take in his family company. Credit is a form of time, the delay in its repayment that enabled him to make the purchase faster. Second, this given time underpinned the market value of American grain. Hammer did not just get the grain, he also did so at a particular moment in time when the grain was at its lowest price given the oversupply. If drought had Russia's "fields burned barren," US farmers were meanwhile burning their grain to prevent its price from going further down. Third (and this is the most important for me here), the market value of grain at that moment in time became another kind of value, a gift value, in Hammer's given time.

What kind of value? It is timely, as it seems an instant solution to the problem of hunger. It is not the timeliness of trade but of hunger alleviation, a moral act of giving life. During Hammer's meeting with Lenin later in 1921, Lenin said, struggling to stop a tear in his eye, that for the grain he wished to "add my humble thanks on behalf of my government" to the "gratitude of these agonized people" (Hammer and Lyndon 1987: 116). After this meeting, Lenin wrote a favorable note about him to the Central Committee of the Communist Party. The note introduced Hammer, described this deal to supply grain in exchange for the Ural valuables with "only" a 5 percent commission. Lenin added that the first thing Armand Hammer did after he arrived in Russia was to "gift surgical equipment worth of $60,000 to Semashko," the People's Commissar for Healthcare (Lenin 1981, vol. 53: 257). Years later, a Kremlin Museum tour guide described Hammer as the "American busi-nessman who delivered the first shipment of wheat flour to the starving peo-ple of Russia" (Bruk 1964: 9). In other words, Soviet documents closely link this grain supply with the gift of surgical equipment, adding to their register the personal gift to Lenin of the *Eritis sicut deus* figurine (Kharitonova 1980: 97–98). In doing so, they put this act of giving time and giving grain into the language of the gift.

The value in question is not just a market but also gift value of grain or monetary value of surgical equipment. Both market and gift time values form interrelated "regimes of value" (Appadurai 1986). They are interrelated because the differences between them are linked when a commodity (grain) becomes a gift, even if this transformation is not the same for all parties involved. Grain became a gift for the Soviet side but, as I demonstrate below, not necessarily for Hammer. But from the point of view of the anthropology of value (Appadurai 1986; Graeber 2001), this is not a problem in itself. Meanings of exchange—for example, if this is a gift or commodity exchange—could be themselves subjects to exchange (Ssorin-Chaikov 2000).

But both gift or commodity exchanges have their own temporalities. The timeliness of Hammer's act is interesting. The supply of grain that he arranged in August 1921 of course did not instantly arrive in the Urals. In fact, this did not happen as speedily as promised but over winter, after it arrived in Petrograd in December 1921 (Hammer and Lyndon 1987: 132). Furthermore, its delivery to famine-struck regions was hampered by the same kind of delays as Hammer's own trip to Moscow and the Urals. But despite these delays, this gift of time immediately generated what I would call this action's *gift effects*. During train stops later that August, "the American who sent a telegram to New York ordering grain for the Urals" was met with huge enthusiasm and applause. He was invited to make public speeches. And Lenin, after he found out about the deal, telegraphed the head of the expedition, Ludvig Martens, to bring the group back to Moscow. When Hammer returned, he was invited to a meeting (Hammer and Lyndon 1987: 109–14).

It is in these events that the credit that Hammer took became a gift to Soviet Russia. The gift of credit gave time to nongift and nonmarket temporalities that he saw and described—the temporalities of endless delays and after-war chaos. But this gift of credit here included gift credit that Hammer received by giving this gift. This time is a gift effect of his act that came earlier than the arrival of the gift itself—that is, the grain. This gift also gave time to itself. It worked as a gift not merely despite but also, in August 1921, *before* its own subsequent delays.

Let's sum up. First, the matter that was being given is time. Second, this time was simultaneously many different times. It was the time of the gift, but also the time of credit, the time of the market in the United States, and the time of possible Soviet futures. (Note that the US grain market was a classic site for the invention of trade in futures, as its prices were set before harvest [Zaloom 2006]). But this identity of different times also happened in the context of multiple temporalities of the time of crisis, visible in the industrial and infrastructural chaos in the aftermath of the Russian Civil War, and the ecological time of peasant agriculture, caught by drought. Other factors to consider are the ecological and market time of American farming, the personal time of the beginning of Hammer's own business, and something I will detail later in this chapter—the emerging market time of the Soviet New Economic Policies, which was also instituted in 1921, modifying the Soviet "red guard assault of the capital" and encouraging substantial elements of market economy within Soviet society.

It may seem that the difference between slowness and speed is just a matter of tempo. Surely, there are different rhythms that can be put side by side within a frame that, as Henri Lefebvre suggests, makes an event or a location analytically similar to a page of a music score. The question is if this "rhythmanalysis" (Lefebvre 2004) is an analysis of different rhythms of the same time. I argue that there are not just multiple rhythms but multiple temporalities that are visible in this tempo. In Hammer's trip and in this grain episode, it is through this given time that we can see a temporal multiplicity, which is as diverse and complex as I outlined in the previous chapter. This temporal multiplicity takes place at a different time—in the wake of the Soviet project rather than in its aftermath. But in this chapter, I also use it analytically for a different purpose. This chapter does not focus on the question of which of the different temporal frameworks *in fact* underpins the events. Instead, it is about how these different temporalities operate together, and as resources for each other. If the previous chapter focused on relations of *change* between temporalities, here I illustrate relations of *exchange* between them.

By exchange I mean that the event of credit (a form of market time) that Hammer *takes* becomes an event within the Soviet time frame, and that this becoming is a matter of *given* time and gift time. The Soviet state, in its historicity (the time of crisis) and its language of help and gift, *takes* Hammer's time. This, in turn, becomes an event within the time frame of Hammer's business. Lenin does not simply offer him an opportunity to do business in Soviet Russia, but also gives him emergency powers to cut through the delay-ridden bureaucratic system. This possibility of speedy action is also a form of time *given*, by Lenin, to Hammer's emerging business. Giving here is allowing; taking is using. Each temporality draws on others, but each does so without erasing or assimilating the other.

Let me go back to the analogy with Marx' conceptualization of exchange that I introduced in chapter 1. If grain is exchanged for iron, there is something common in both. In the moment of exchange, these two things are equivalent to one another. But at the same time they are not equivalent, because if they were, there would be no need for exchange. Equivalence here is only a way to express difference, which is not erased but maintained in this relation of identity. Marx famously went on to question this identity expressed in exchange value. He suggests that this difference is in the labor value of these goods, which was, for him, time: labor time. It is grain-making labor time that is exchanged for iron-making labor time, and at the moment of exchange, the two are both identical and different. They are identical as abstract labor. But they are different in terms of use values, since labor as skill is different for each commodity. What we see in Hammer's grain deal and other episodes that follow in this chapter are exchanges between market time, gift time, and state time. They appear identical at the moment of exchange, but only to express difference.

The situation with which I have started, in which the market value of grain at a given moment in time becomes the gift value of Hammer's given time, highlights a very different kind of relation within this temporal multiplicity in comparison to what I described in the previous chapter. Here, gift time equals market time in relations of *exchange*, which works very differently from a one-time *change* into another. In change, the temporality of a given practice was thought to be X, but is in fact not X but Y. In X —> Y, X is Y, but Y is not X (in mathematical terms, it is not "commutative"). In contrast, in exchange, X = Y and Y = X. There is no linear progress from one meaning of time to the other, but trade and accumulation on both sides. *Change* is a relation of unbridgeable difference; *exchange* is a relation of identity. But this identity is also a matter of time in two senses: X = Y and Y = X, first, at the moment of exchange, and second, they are not necessarily to be given in the same moment. It is temporal delay and remedy thereof in this case that is constitutive of equivalence and their exchange value. This means that X = Y and Y = X is itself time. If X and Y were really the same, there would be no need of exchange.

I have introduced this chapter with the example of the Hammer's gift of grain and his gift of time. But the rest on the chapter focuses on another of Hammer's gifts, the sculpture *Eritis sicut deus* (see fig. 1, p. xiv). My concern in discussing this gift will be the identity *and* difference between or among the time of the market, the time of the gift, and the time of the state—the situation of the X =/≠ Y and Y =/≠ X—in which X = Y and Y = X only at the moment of exchange. I will proceed by asking what exactly is this *moment of exchange*. In chapter 1, I used Alfred Gell (1992) to introduce these formal relationships as sequences of events. But, as Mark Hodges perceptively noted, one of the problems with this perspective, which originates in the analytical philosophy of time, is that events have fuzzy boundaries. "When does an 'event' begin?" is a crucial question here (Hodges 2008: 405). I will show that there are two competing chronologies of this gift, which are important for understanding when the *event* of Hammer's visit of Russia began, exactly when he gave the *Eritis sicut deus* sculpture, what it was in sequence of events of his visit, and what are the relations between gift and market time. Therefore, another correlation that is charted here is the one between these temporalities of exchange and chronological linear time.

Gift time

Time has been central to the conceptualization of the gift. But this conceptualization was driven by a specter of the market—that is, by the question of to what extent the explanation of the gift reduces it to the market-like logic of economic exchange. Marcel Mauss argues that gifts create obligations to reciprocate, and the gift imposes an obligatory time limit to reciprocate as itself a form of reciprocity—the "guarantee" that it will happen (Mauss 2016: 114). Pierre Bourdieu does not question this "surety," but argues that if this time limit is understood mechanically, then it transforms gift into market. Setting up a precise moment of time after which it is too late to reciprocate makes the gift into credit. This moment would remain invisible, however, if we reciprocate at the "right moment," which does not have a precise temporal location. Credit is made visible when we are late, which leaves the receiving party to think that countergift is there just because of this obligation. Obligation is also visible when we are too early. If the gift is immediately reciprocated, this amounts to a rejection of the initial gift: "Overmuch eagerness to discharge one's obligation," says Bourdieu, quoting La Rochefoucauld, "is a form of ingratitude": "To betray one's haste to be free of an obligation one has incurred, and thus to reveal too overtly one's desire to pay off services rendered or gifts received, to be quits, is to denounce the initial gift retrospectively as motivated by the intention of obliging one" (Bourdieu 1991: 105).

The art of gift giving is thus the art of timing the gift, when it is reciprocated neither too early nor too late, so that the economism of reciprocity does not become explicit. But, as Jacques Derrida argues, even trying to make reciprocity *not explicit* actually installs it. For him, the very same temporality that Mauss' gift creates also destroys it. It is this "temporalization," that is, this anticipation, memory, retention, and protention, and the immanence of the future that reduces the gift to the return: "The simple identification of the passage of a gift as such, that is, of an identifiable thing among some identifiable 'ones,' would be nothing other than the destruction of the gift. It is as if, between the event of the institution of gift as such and its destruction, the difference were destined to be constantly annulled. At the limit, the gift as gift ought not to appear as gift: either to the donee or to the donor" (Derrida 1992: 14).

But this line of gift theory proceeds on assumptions that first, there exists such a thing as the gift "as such"; second, that the time of this gift is singular; and third, that this time can be understood either by analogy with the time of the market or by contrast with it. My argument in this chapter will be that all this is not the case. The episode with which I started this chapter centers on the event of one of Hammer's gifts. But before I continue with the other events of his Russian trip and the gift of *Eritis sicut deus*, some remarks on the narrative about these events need to be made.

Narrative time

Hammer's own memoirs are the source for the travel episodes that I recount here. They describe the very beginning of his multimillionaire wealth. He writes that this Russian trip was a turning point for a medical student's decision to become a businessman. This could be seen as a transformative event or rupture in a sense explicated by Alain Badiou (2005). In Ekaterinburg, Hammer was admittedly still thinking about humanitarianism, and about his medical career in the long run; it was Lenin, whom Hammer met in October, who convinced him to turn to business. After that meeting, from the first trade deal to ship grain to Russia and a first concession, hashed out with Lenin, to develop asbestos mining in the Urals, Hammer's wealth grew as he became involved in the manufacturing of pencils in the Soviet Union for world-wide sale later in the 1920s, the export of nationalized art from Russian collections, alcohol trading in the United States during the Depression, and subsequently the oil business.

What exactly, then, is *gift time* in Hammer's autobiographical narrative of his wealth? This question is important, as it is this gift of time where the narrative of his wealth really starts. We see this narrative rooted in virtues of humanitarianism and in the speed of his own thinking and business intuition—in gifts that he gives and in the gift that he has. But this is a *retrospective* narrative of his business success, written much later, in the 1980s, and very much in defense of the morality of his wealth. Relations with the Soviet Union of course bring a particular twist to this story of wealth, but as narrative it is not exceptional in its genre. This is what I would call capital's mythical origin time; it is a story that capital tells about itself in a form of a capitalist's autobiography.

This mythical origin time is morally ambiguous no matter whether such stories are told by nineteenth-century robber barons or twentieth-first-century information technology millionaires. Hammer's humanitarian motivation can be, and indeed was, questioned from the very start. In the United States, he was suspected of being a communist, particularly as he came from a communist family and later channeled Soviet funding for the Comintern and the US Communist Party. J. Edgar Hoover systematically spied on him from the time of his

1921 trip (Blumay and Edwards 1992; Epstein 1996; Weinberg 1992). In the Soviet Union, Hammer was officially praised as a great "friend" but he became increasingly controversial as his role in Soviet trade of art that was confiscated from the Hermitage and other Russian collections in the late 1920s and 1930s became publicly known. In post–Soviet Russia, impressions of him became compromised as directly benefiting from selling Hermitage and other Russian "art for tractors" (Odom and Salmond 2009).

But, of course, it is unsurprising that the narrative of theft appears as the flip side of the narrative of gift in capital's mythical origin time. This other side has, however, a complex history that includes none other than the very narrative of "primitive accumulation" in Marx' *Capital*, which became foundational for the Soviet order. Perhaps in other circumstances, Hammer's business could have become part of this story, as primitive accumulation is not simply morally ambiguous but also not completely capitalist. It conforms the narrative of the history of capital as continuously dispossessive and extortionate (see, for example, Harvey 2005; Graeber 2011; Sassen 2014), resourcing capitalism's nonmarket outside. (Indeed, for Marx, the period of "primitive accumulation" was this nonmarket outside, as capitalist market economy did not yet exist during this period.)

These multiple recursions of the time of the gift and capital are further complicated by the fact that Hammer's gift of time and his other gifts, including his personal gift to Lenin, were reassembled into another gift economy altogether. *With all one's heart*, the catalog of gifts to Lenin in the Museum of Lenin's Kremlin Flat, spells this out:

> On October 22, 1921, Lenin received Armand Hammer, a representative of an allied American corporation producing medicines and chemical products, to discuss the leasing of the first concessions in the Soviet republic and the delivery of one million poods of wheat on favourable terms to the famine-stricken Volga area and the Urals.
>
> In Lenin's study there is a small bronze monkey presented to Lenin by Hammer in memory of the meeting.
>
> Gifts to Lenin from foreign representatives show the affection and respect of the working people of various countries for the creator of the world's first socialist state and for the leader of the world communist movement. Some of them tell us about the sources of business connections of the young Soviet republic with representatives of the countries which had a wish to cooperate with the Land of the Soviets. (Kharitonova 1980: 97–98)

Note that American farmers do not appear in this narrative as selling grain for a market price at that time when it hits its lowest because the supply is high. The so-called favorable terms of the grain supply imply more than humanitarian reasons: international solidarity in response not merely to the crisis but also to the Soviet gift of new time—to the new dawn of history that the Soviet order claimed to be.

Chronological time

In short, as there are *multiple gifts* contained in Hammer's gift of time in late summer of 1921, when he "got an idea" that his quick credit could save lives, there are also *multiple times* in his gift to Lenin. If gift time is here a pivot in relations of exchange between different temporalities, then a "small bronze monkey," Hugo Wolfgang Rheinhold's *Eritis sicut deus*, is a pivot of this pivot. This is because *Eritis sicut deus* does not merely convey different meanings of time, which I introduced in chapter 1—the Christian, Darwinist, and Marxist "you will be as gods." It also, as it happens, presents a timing problem, as there exist two competing chronologies as to when this gift was given. The Museum of Lenin's Flat in the Kremlin lists October 22, 1921, as the gift date, and it also indicates this as the time of single meeting of Lenin and Hammer (Kunetskaia and Mashtakova 1979: 151; Shubina 2006: 213). Historians of Soviet-American relations and Hammer's biographers, however, usually mention two meetings (Weinberg 1992: 49; Gillette 1981; Epstein 1996), in the autumn of 1921 and in spring of 1922; *Eritis sicut deus* was given to Lenin during the second meeting. These dates are based on Hammer's own memoirs. Paradoxically, in his 1965 interview to the *Soviet Life* magazine, Hammer also speaks of a single visit (Bruk 1964).

This slippage in chronology indicates different ways in which the gift time of Hammer's visit works as a point of exchange relations between temporalities of the emerging Soviet state. There are at least three different ways to understand these relationships, which I consider in sections below. I will tell—or, rather, retell—three stories of the same events of August–October 1921, from different points of view. I will be interested in a relationship between a singularity and multiplicity: a singularity of "gift" in gift event, the singularity of "event" in gift event, and in multiplicity of these gifts and events. I argue that the decomposition of this singularity into multiple parts (Strathern 1991) does not merely indicate the composite nature of the gift time but also exchanges the gift time with another matter altogether: it places it into commodity time and state time.

Hammer's gift

In 1964, the president of Occidental Petroleum, Armand Hammer, visited the USSR as part of a delegation of US businessmen to discuss possibilities of trade. At the trade conference in Moscow, Soviet Novosti Press Agency correspondent Mikhail Bruk was waiting in the hotel lobby looking for opportunities to glean any information about what might have been going on behind the closed doors. He wondered if Hammer, listed on the program, was "the son of the famous Hammer who met and talked with Lenin half a century ago." At a coffee break, he approached Hammer with this question and was "nonplussed" (Bruk 1964: 9) to find out that the American businessman was not Hammer's son or relative, but Hammer himself.

They agreed to an interview in which Hammer told the story of his visit. But Hammer did this through another story. Another "funny thing," another misrecognition, had apparently happened to him just the previous day. A tour guide had taken him and other Americans, after their meeting with the then Soviet Premier Alexei Kosygin, to the Museum of Lenin's Flat in the Kremlin. During the tour, the guide pointed to a small statue of a bronze monkey and described that this was a gift from an "American businessman who delivered the first shipment of wheat flour to the starving people of Russia."

"I believe his name is Hammer," she said, "but I am sure he must be dead by now." Hammer exclaimed, "I am very much alive!" The guide asked him to tell the story of this meeting, and it is *this* story that Hammer repeats to Mikhail Bruk:

> I was 23 then and a medical doctor. But business always appealed to me more than medicine, and I came to Soviet Russia back in 1921 to see what business prospects there were in your country. The primary aim of my trip to Moscow was to negotiate a concession from the Soviet Government, probably somewhere in the Urals. Somebody told me that Lenin was very fond of *objets d'art*. And so I decided, in case I should meet him, to present him with some kind of antique. In London I came across a bronze monkey in an antique shop. It struck my fancy and I bought it and brought it with me to Moscow. I also brought with me a set of equipment for a hospital that was to be built in your country and tuned it over to Mr. Nikolai Semashko, then People's Commissar for Health, who offered me a trip to the Urals while the equipment is being installed. (Bruk 1964: 9)

This story significantly diverges from the one that Hammer gave in his memoirs, which he subsequently published. We see here that his interests were in business and not humanitarianism, although the latter is the story that the tour guide told to the visitors of Lenin's flat.

There is a singular date of this meeting. There is a composite singularity of the gift of the bronze statue, the medical equipment, "the first shipment of wheat flour to the starving people of Russia," and Hammer's business proposals. All are given as one. There is even a narrative singularity of this story in the Soviet English-language *Soviet Life* magazine, published under the title "He talked to Lenin." It is concise, just one-page long, a picture-like text accompanied by a photo of Hammer holding the statue in the center of group of American businessmen. There is also a singularity of focus in composition of this photo. "American business leaders in Lenin's Kremlin study," as it is entitled (see fig. 3), all look at the statue, which is in Hammer's hands while it is only Hammer who looks at the camera. The singularity of the gift and the giver is the mirror of the singularity of the absent receiver. If the recipient were there, all eyes would be on him. But now, at this singular moment, the center is Hammer: "He talked to Lenin."

American business leaders in Lenin's Kremlin study. Dr. Armand Hammer holds the figure that he presented to Lenin 44 years ago.

Figure 3. "American business leaders in Lenin's Kremlin study," 1964. *Soviet Life Magazine.*

This singularity, composite as it is, centers nonetheless on a single meeting date: October 22, 1921. I have already mentioned that this chronological singularity is disputed, but it is important that it is fixed in this way in this particular story as well as in other Soviet documents. This event's singularity works for two related temporalities. First, there is *museum time*, which is about preserving such singularities for eternity. To tell this story, Hammer sits down with the tour guide "at the very same desk" and "in the same room"; Hammer emphasizes that it has been preserved in exactly the way it was when Lenin was there last. That time is the event and eternity of this museum time: the clock hands in Lenin's

study show 8:15. This was the time in the evening of December 12, 1922, when
he agreed to doctor's advice to move from the Kremlin to Gorki, a countryside
estate near Moscow, from where he never returned to the Kremlin to work
before his death in 1924. The museum preserves, in the frame of this singularity, both the time of Lenin's work and life, which includes the routine time of
his meetings with the government and party colleagues and the unique times
of individual visits, of which science fiction writer H. G. Wells' visit is often
mentioned as the most iconic.

Second, this singularity formats the *meaning of the gift*. Hammer is careful
to put this meaning not in his own words but in those of Soviet recipients. It
is the tour guide who describes him as the "American businessman who delivered the first shipment of wheat flour to the starving people of Russia." In
the same interview, he mentions that a car driver who chauffeured him to see
Soviet politician Anostas Mikoyan, whom Hammer knew from the 1920s, told
him on the way back to the hotel: "Mr. Hammer, I just found out that you
are the well-known pencil manufacturer. Soon after the October Revolution
in Russia you taught us how to make pencils so that we, the illiterate people of
Russian, learn to write. And now we make sputniks and rockets that we send
to the moon." He is asked if he agrees with H. G. Wells, who described Lenin
as "the Kremlin dreamer." Hammer states that the car driver's words, "now we
make sputniks and rockets that we send to the moon" are the best answer to
that question. "Some 30 years ago I gave H. G. Wells, whom I knew quite well,
the first automatic pencil made by our factory. Pity he is dead now. Otherwise
I would tell him that he underestimated Lenin and your country" (Bruk 1964:
9). In the Soviet narrative, which we see Hammer using here, even help such
as wheat flour to save Russia from hunger or pencils made in to teach Russians
to write were merely generous responses to something else. That "something
else" is what really released Russia's potential—the power of communist ideas,
embodied in the figure of the "Kremlin's dreamer." His gifts are countergifts of
"affection and respect of the working people of various countries for the creator of the world's first socialist state and for the leader of the world communist
movement" (Kharitonova 1980: 98).

In the narrative that these gifts tell, "the Kremlin dreamer" does not refer
to living in fantasies like H. G. Wells' science fiction, but to his agency in making dreams a reality. This dreamer's action is a gift of time—of drawing a line
between a B-series (Gell 1992) distinction of "before" and "after," dreams and
reality. This is the gift that the Museum of Lenin's Kremlin Flat celebrates. This

temporality, as with all the temporality I discuss in this chapter, is place-specific. This is "chronotope" in Mikhail Bakhtin's original meaning of the term, that is, the unity of time and space specific to a particular *narrative* (Bakhtin 1975)—here, the narrative of the 1964 interview or the narrative of the catalog of the Museum of Lenin's Kremlin Flat. This Kremlin museum, and not just its catalog, tells the story of a place in which the *new world as new time* was conceived. The revolutionary action to overthrow the Provisional Government—the one that ruled Russia between February and October 1917, that is, between the February Revolution that led to the abdication of Tsar Nicholas II, and the Bolshevik taking power—took place in Petrograd (St. Petersburg). It is marked there by Lenin's monument, where he spoke from the armored car at the Baltic Railway Station, having arrived from exile, and the memorial plaque at the Smol'nyi Institute, the revolutionary headquarters that he chaired. In contrast, Lenin's flat in the Kremlin is a monument to Lenin's *thought*; its full name is "The Museum of Lenin's Flat *and Study* [my emphasis]." It shows where the Soviet power and government materialized from thought to reality, and where the reality of world history, hitherto marked by exploitation and injustice, is beginning to be transformed into a Soviet "dreamworld" (Buck-Morss 2000). Lenin's library there, which includes many gifted books, includes a copy of *The glow in the abyss* by Henri Barbusse (1920), signed "to Lenin who first wrote down the great unwritten laws, with great admiration," and a copy of Ivan Kasatkin's *Forest true stories* (1919) with a dedication, "To Vladimir Il'ich Ulianov (Lenin), Who mightily moved hard forest reality into dream [tale]" (see figs. 4 and 5).

This dreamworld perspective operates in retrospective *commemorative time*, which goes into production after Lenin's death in 1924 (Dickerman 2001; Tumarkin 1987; Yurchak 2015). This particular museum form of commemorative time reaches completion when, in 1955, the Museum of Lenin's Kremlin Flat is created, and the Kremlin as a museum opens to the public. Gifts that are on display there—books and objects from various visitors—are about the singularity of the event of the beginning of the Soviet order. From this point of view, precise dates of these gifts and gift events are not as important—as they demarcate broader and singular distinctions of *before* and *after*. The *Eritis sicut deus* figurine depicts the substitution of the world after Darwin with the world after Marx.

Here, the singularity of the meeting between Hammer and Lenin stands for this singularity of this epic change. The historic division in its totality as the beginning of the new world metonymically absorbs other events, to the point of events that are relevant to the time of narration rather than the time that is

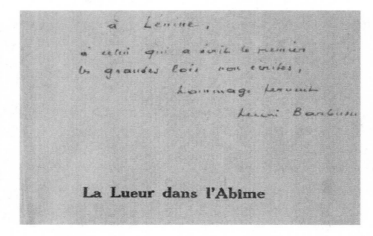

Figure 4. "To Lenin who first wrote down the great unwritten laws, with great admiration." Dedication of Henri Barbusse of his *Le lueur dans l'abime [The glow in the abyss]* (Paris 1920), as a gift to V. I. Lenin. *Courtesy of the Museum of Lenin's Flat and Study, Gorki Leninskie.*

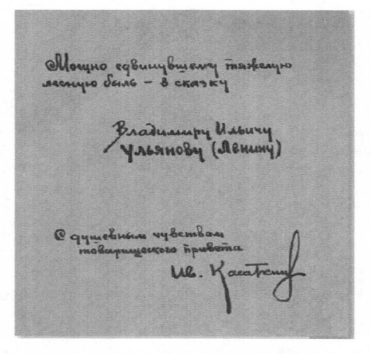

Figure 5. "To Vladimir Il'ich Ulianov (Lenin), Who mightily moved hard forest reality into dream [tale]." Dedication of Ivan Kasatkin of his *Forest true stories* (Moscow 1919), as a gift to V. I. Lenin. *Courtesy of the Museum of Lenin's Flat and Study, Gorki Leninskie.*

narrated. "I tell him [Lenin]," Hammer describes in 1964 of his 1921 meeting, "'This is an illustration of Darwin's theory." "No," Lenin replies, "This is clearly an allegory. The artist wants to convey that, if peoples of the world do not learn to live in peace, with the development of new forms of arms, only monkeys will survive to play with man's skulls." In chapter 1, I discussed this gift's aesthetics in terms of the Darwinian and Marxist upturning of Christian creationist narratives. But here Lenin seems to be outside the logics that I draw out: Lenin laughed but added seriously, "coexistence [rather than war] is essential, particularly between Soviet Russia and the United States" (Bruk 1964: 9).

Yet this meaning falls in a place in the museum time. In this description, Lenin's reading of the meaning of the gift as an allegory of the dangers of an arms race sits more easily with the realities of the 1960s than the 1920s. Donna Haraway (1989) remarked on the ease in which Darwinist primatology was being used allegorically to think about the Cold War in the 1960s. Indeed, it is this Khrushchev's "thaw" in the Cold War, not Lenin's New Economic Policies, that has enabled Hammer's and other US businessmen's visit of the USSR. The "coexistence . . . particularly between Soviet Russia and the United States" evokes "peaceful coexistence" (*mirnoe sosushchestvovanie*) and "discharging" or easing of tensions (*razriadka napriazhennosti*)—in other words, the vocabulary of the nuclear arms race and of diplomatic exchanges between the United States and the USSR after the Cuban crisis. Hammer's point (in 1964) is that Lenin could foresee such dangerous developments; the dreamworld that transpired in the 1920s contained, in gift form, configurations of the future. It is as if in the Wilsonian détente Lenin could see the coming of the Cold War world order. Realities of the 1960s are in this perspective within the singularity of the beginning of the bipolar world of "the short twentieth century" (Hobsbawm 1995) as a periodization of competition of socialist and capitalist mass utopias from 1914 to 1991.

Lenin's gift

Let me now turn to the second chronology of these gift events. It includes two meetings of Hammer and Lenin. This chronology is based on Hammer's 1987 memoirs. After the deal to swap grain for valuables was made, in early Autumn 1921, the trip continued until the train was stopped by the news that Lenin wished to have a conversation with Ludvig Martens, a professional revolutionary and mining engineer who coordinated the trip. As there was no telephone connection available, this conversation took the form of an exchange of tel-egrams in real time. Martens invited Hammer and another American to the railway station telegraph with him, and after a long exchange between Martens and Lenin about the situation in the Urals, Hammer was surprised to see his name on the ticker-tape: "What is this we hear from the Ekaterinburg ROSTA [Russian Telegraph Agency] about a young American chartering grain ships for the relief famine in the Urals?" "It is correct," replied Martens: "Dr. Armand Hammer has instructed his associates in New York to send grain immediately to Petrograd on the understanding, which has been approved by the Ekaterin-burg Soviet, that a return cargo of furs and other goods would be taken back to cover the costs of grain shipment." Lenin asked, "Do you personally approve this?" "Yes, I highly recommend this," Martens replied, smiling at Hammer. "Very good," Lenin concluded the exchange, "I will order the Foreign Trade Monopoly Department to confirm the transaction. Please return to Moscow immediately" (Hammer and Lyndon 1987: 111).

In Moscow, Hammer was invited to a meeting with Lenin. It was after this meeting that Lenin wrote the favorable note about him to the Central Committee of the Communist Party, which I have mentioned in the opening of this chapter. The note introduced Armand Hammer as a son "of American millionaire [Julius] Hammer" who was at that time in prison, allegedly for as-sisting an illegal abortion, "but in fact for his Communist views." Then Lenin went on to describe a deal to supply grain in exchange for the Ural valuables with "only 5 percent commission." Furthermore, added Lenin, the first thing Hammer did after he arrived in Russia was to "gift surgical equipment worth of $60,000 to Semashko," the People's Commissar for Healthcare (Lenin 1981: 257). To oversee the deal, Hammer returned to Russia in 1922. This time, he requested an audience with Lenin and gave him the gift of *Eritis sicut deus*, which he had purchased in a London antique shop (Hammer and Lyndon 1987: 139).

The meanings of this exchange in the context of the idioms of Communism and its international support can be found in Lenin's note when he mentions Hammer's communist background and that the commission is "only" 5 percent. But, as I argued above, this idiom is contingent on the singularity of the gift event, and of the single meeting of Lenin and Hammer. The question is this: does adding another event—the second meeting in 1922—and the attribution of the event of gifting *Eritis sicut deus* to this second meeting still add up to the same picture? I argue that this dissembling of the binary of before and after into a more detailed chronology complicates the meaning of this gift-event so that it can be reassembled in more than one way.

Hammer's memoirs not only introduce the second meeting but also change the meaning of this gift exchange in his account of the first meeting. In this regard, his 1987 account is very different from the story he gave in 1964. In his 1987 memoirs, he describes how he arrived in the Kremlin in October 1921 via Trinity Gates, how he had to temporarily leave his passport there in exchange for a single entry pass, how crowded the entry to Lenin's office was. He was taken to Lenin's study, away from the crowd. He noted numerous books, newspapers, and magazines, including a copy of *Scientific American*, which Lenin showed to him, when he led the conversation to the topic of American progress: "Look here," Lenin told Hammer, "this is what your people have done. This is what progress means: buildings, inventions, machines, development of mechanical aid to human hands." Lenin compared Russia's new historic time to America at the "pioneer age": "We need the knowledge and the spirit that made America what she is today"; the United States and Russia complement one another as Russia is a "backward" country with undeveloped natural resources, and America could find here a market for machines and eventually for industrial commodities (Hammer and Lyndon 1987: 116).

For the grain that will be delivered to alleviate famine, Lenin said, "To the gratitude of these agonized people, I add my humble thanks on behalf of my government." After a pause of silence, when Hammer thinks Lenin struggled to stop a tear in his eye, he added: "What we really need . . . is American capital and technical aid to get our wheels turning once more. . . . New Economic Policy demands a fresh development of our economic possibilities. We hope to accelerate this process by a system of industrial and commercial concessions to foreigners. It will give great opportunities to the United States. Have you thought of that at all?" Hammer replied that one of his travel companions, a mining engineer, tried to interest him in asbestos mines in Alepayevsk, in the Urals, but added that he did not wish to take up more of Lenin's time with his personal matters. "No at all," said Lenin in response, "this is not the point. Someone must break the ice. Why don't you take this asbestos concession yourself?"

Hammer was astonished. He understood this, he writes, as "a historic opportunity Lenin was offering me." In his account of this Russian trip, he stressed time and time again that until that point he thought about his visit purely in humanitarian terms. This was a turning point, almost a gift-event—an event of Lenin's gift of a business offer—in which humanitarianism became business, although Hammer acknowledges that the *turning point of this turning point* was his earlier brilliant idea of taking credit to supply grain in exchange for the valuables, which opened the door for this opportunity. He replied to Lenin that, given the *slowness* of ways in which such things are done in Soviet Russia, even preliminary negotiations might take months. To this, Lenin said that he understood that bureaucracy was one of "our curses" and offered to set up a commission of two people, one from the Workers' and Peasants' Inspectorate, and the other from the All-Russian Emergency Committee (the CheKa, which is the precursor to the KGB) to oversee the project. "You may rest assured that they will act promptly. It shall be done at once." Hammer notes that he witnessed "the embryo" of the Soviet Concessions Committee (1987: 117–18), which subsequently put the temporality of foreign business in Russia at a very different rhythm than Soviet Russia's own industry and bureaucracy.

Hammer gives the gift of time when he takes credit to ship the grain, which is here matched not merely with Lenin's business offer but also with Lenin's gift of time, which is to be saved in setting up and running this concession. Yet Lenin's gift of time does not reciprocate Hammer's gift of time. It follows it. It is given *after* Lenin expresses his "humble thanks" on behalf on the government for Hammer's gift, in addition "to the gratitude of these agonized people." Lenin finishes with the gratitude, closes this topic, and goes to business. But Lenin's given time in his business offer is not a giving of market time—as it was in the case of grain—but of state time. This is the offer of speedy and resolute state support for this project by merger of an institution of class warfare and class control, Workers' and Peasants' Inspectorate (*RABKRIN, Raboche-Krestianskaia Inspektsiia*), and the terror power of the Soviet security services. This is empathetically a giving of time: Hammer can rest assured all will be done promptly, "at once." There is a popular but unconfirmed story, also attributed to Hammer, that at that meeting he also received a note from Lenin that stated, "Whoever presents this should be let in to see me *at any time*—V. I. Ulianov-Lenin, 1921" (Zhirnov 2000; my emphasis). According to this story, he used this document once during a visit to Moscow's Red Square when he claimed to have wished to see Lenin's Mausoleum at night. The astonished guard, having recognized Lenin's signature, let him in.

What is the meaning of the gift of the *Eritis sicut deus* sculpture, then, if it was not given at this meeting in 1921 but at the next one in 1922, that is, if Hammer purchased this statue *after* he returned to New York to forge the development of these new business links, and when he embarked on his second trip to Soviet Russia in the spring of 1922? This meaning is not in the frame of a singular gift-event that separates the before and after in the foundational metanarrative of the Soviet time. It is an event in a line of events that start with Hammer's gift of surgical equipment, continues with the offer of American grain, and with Lenin's business offer. Its frame, then, is not so much a metanarrative as a microhistorcial division of several befores and afters. This is a temporality of the beginning of business relations, with their own cycles of reciprocity, which are quite different from the reciprocity of Maussian gift theory. It implies a pragmatic political and business time in which the *Eritis sicut deus* gift expresses Hammer's gratitude to Lenin for his business offer, and cements their personal relations as a guarantor of Hammer's business' state of exception in Soviet Russia.

This temporality is, however, not merely that of historical, matter-of-fact temporal order that Alfred Gell associates with B-series, "just a row of events strung together, like the beads on a necklace" (Gell 1992: 151). These microhistorical divisions of before and after, into which we see the metanarrative of Soviet before and after divided, also add up to other time frames more akin to an A-series, with perceptually different notions of past, present, and future.

Given that this business starts with gifts of the surgical equipment and the gift of time during Hammer's trip to the Urals, and then, already as business, is cemented with *Eritis sicut deus*, this is a complex transformation of gift into business. This change is a distinct story that is embedded in perceptually different notions of past, present, and future for both Hammer and Lenin, although in different ways. Given Lenin's open admiration of "American progress," which is visible not only in what he says to Hammer and the copies of *Scientific American* in his Kremlin office but also in his well-known appreciation of the US industrial organization, such as Fordism, which Lenin sought to emulate, then it becomes increasingly ambiguous who, in these Soviet-American exchanges, gives gifts to whom. In light of these exchanges, it is clear that *Eritis sicut deus* is not just a gift of gratitude for Russia's gift to the world: the gift of the Revolution. Is this merely a gift of Hammer's personal gratitude to Lenin in response to this business offer? Or is it a token of the American gift of modernity to Russia, of which other parts include the American hunger relief to the Volga river area and Western concessions that Hammer wants to set up and that are to jump-start Russia's industrialization and modernization after the chaos and devastation of the Civil War?

No matter who gives these gifts to whom, however, this is a gift of progress, or what I call "the gift of modernity." This is not a Maussian gift that reproduces sociality. It is the disruptive gift of "time-forward" that Lenin articulates both when he is trying to convince his foreign visitors, such as H. G. Wells, that he is building an entirely new world, and when he sells Hammer a vision of Soviet Russia as once again in America's "pioneer age," opening up a land of opportunities. However, the contrast with Mauss is not simply of the cyclical time of reciprocity versus linear or spiral, dialectical time of progress, which Lenin wished to achieve with the help of Hammer and other business concessionaires, and market relations of the New Economic Policies. Lenin's thinking is much closer to nineteenth-century ideas of progress than Mauss' at the time of his writing on the gift. *The gift* was written in the context of Mauss' disillusionment with modernity and its progress that was a result of the First World War. But it also followed the fin de siècle and the early twentieth-century cultural mood of archaism and nostalgia, decay and decadence (M. Anderson 1992; Noll and Segal 1994; Fournier 2006; Hart 2014), in which the Darwinian aesthetics of *Eritis sicut deus* (circa 1893) was also quite exceptional,[1] if not simply backward.

The temporary, the urgent, and the emerging: The new time

"A few words on Lenin's impetuosity," writes Ludvig Martens (1875–1948) of his meetings and correspondence with Lenin, "his handwritten notes and letters replete with words such as 'urgently,' 'super-urgently' [*arkhispeshno*], 'very urgently,' often underlined two or three times" (1958: 148). These are his remarks on Lenin's exchanges with Hammer:

> In front of me there is a note, dated November 17, 1921, in which I let Lenin know that the first ship with the grain, as agreed with the American concessionaires, is leaving New York. . . . Lenin writes back on it that I should let Peter [Petrograd] and Foreign Trade [Commissariat] know immediately as without triple checks on this nothing will be ready and we end up falling on our face [*oskandalimsia*]. This note was accompanied by Lenin's characteristic "urgent." (Martens 1958: 148)

Martens knew Lenin through networks of St. Petersburg Marxist coteries from 1894 when Martens was a student at St. Petersburg Technological Institute.

---

1.   I thank Peter Holquist for pointing this out to me.

He joined Lenin's "Union for the Liberation of the Working Class" in 1895, was arrested the next year, and after three-years imprisonment was expelled to Germany, where he competed his engineering degree. He immigrated in 1906 to Britain and to the United States in 1916, before he returned to Russia in 1917. In 1919, he went back to the United States as a head of the Russian Soviet Government Bureau in New York, where he met Hammer. His professional engineering experience, that twice took him to the United States, made him a valuable cadre for planning Soviet industrialization. But as historian of the US communist movement Theodore Draper puts it, it also epitomizes a paradox of mutual gifts of communism between Russia and America, namely that while the "material basis of the Russian Revolution was in America; . . . the political fulfillment of the American economy was in Russia" (2003: 266).

Some of Lenin's own thinking about the American economy is reflected in his correspondence with Martens. But notes exchanged about Hammer reveal a temporality of Soviet construction that is more complex than merely a combination of futures—the Russian political future and the American economic future. There is an all-pervasive temporality of urgency that is highlighted by Lenin's distinct rhythm of work on paper, his inpatient underlining, and in his emergency powers that he is always quick to use—giving Hammer state-of-emergency business help is but one instance of this. It is not, or not just *yet* "an arrhythmia of unpunctuated and irregular now-frenetic, now-idle work" time (Verdery 1996: 57). Rather, it is similar to a Hobbesian temporality, which I outlined in chapter 2. The very acknowledgement, by Lenin, that "without triple checks on this nothing will be ready" evokes a Hobbesian social order, described by Durkheim as "maintained by the act of will that must be constantly renewed" (Durkheim 1960: 136). In America—where Hammer's grain is shipped from—it seems from this point of view that nothing needs to be triple-checked. There, "the economy" (Mitchell 1998) seems to be a true social automaton. On the contrary, the combination of delays and urgency that are ubiquitous from railroads to Commissariats are more than a temporary state of the aftermath of the Civil War. This is the routine state of bureaucratic time that both Hammer and Lenin identify in their conversation. Hammer fears it might impede business; Lenin agrees that this is "one of our curses" and offers a special arrangement to cut through these delays. In other words, this order combines the slow time—with the glimpses of Hobbesian disorder—and the rhythms of quick and forceful interventions.

One of the problems of "the act of will that must be constantly renewed" is not merely that it tends to become routine, precisely because it must be constantly renewed. It is also difficult to identify the time of its beginning. There is a theoretical and philosophical issue of the first will, and there is an ethnographic and historical issue of who claims this role of first, if not key, agent. This is also a temporal reasoning—of *before* and *after*—linking time to agency. I take Carol Greenhouse's point that time is about culturally specific formulation or "distribution of agency"—that is, with broad, varied, and contested meanings that people attach to questions of possibility, causation, and relevance (1996: 82–83). In a particular instance of this chapter's material, the question of agency is a composite question. First, there is the locus of the will—of when and who exactly had a gift of a "brilliant idea" to set up Western concessions in Soviet Russia (in this aspect, the issue of agency is that of ethnocentrically Western modern subjects like Hammer, Martens, and Lenin). Second, there are Marxist notions of historical causality and inevitability where it is history that has agency, rather than an individual subject (although here not *agency* but *hegemony* is an indigenous Marxist term).

Let's start with the first one. This is what Martens says about exchanges between Hammer, Lenin, and himself:

> The above-mentioned American concessionaires were the first ones to receive an industrial concession from us. [During our trip to the Urals] I was able to interest one American company in Alapaevsk asbestos deposits in the Urals. One of the conditions of this concession was the delivery of one million poods of bread to the Urals as soon as possible. (Martens 1958: 148)

The picture of exchanges with Hammer changes again! The whole trip, including the Urals leg, now appears as a part of the Soviet business plan. Hammer's insights, his quick reactions, and gifts of time now appear as expected and desired responses in situations that were carefully framed. The intended outcomes were important economically as well as politically. Martens adds,

> On this issue Vladimir Ilyitch [Lenin] wrote me on October 19, 1921, that, if concessionaire Hammer's plan is serious, we need to put it in precise juridical form of contract or concession. Even if fictional, he [Lenin] wrote, this is a concession nonetheless. It is important for us to show and print [in the newspapers] that the Americans went for concessions—this is politically important. (Martens 1958: 148)

The temporality of these interventions is not of a plan or road map, with clear milestones and goals, but of opportunities that were to be created and seized. There are potentialities for which one needs to stay alert but that are by no means planned. These opportunities are gifts of time in a sense of Jacques Derrida's gift (1992)—that is, something that was not intended to be given, let alone given as gift. These gifts are the time of urgency, the time of "as soon as possible," the time of this creative uncertainly and of agentive, creative action.

Let me turn to the second meaning of agency here. In this temporality of urgency and improvisation, from the point of the revolutionary outside of the existing order of things—the capitalist world order—there is nothing spontaneous that has not been already framed by a Marxist metahistory (cf. White 1973). This metanarrative posits communist future as a temporal horizon that, in turn, creates specific meanings for all things that happened as hitherto history. It has an "iron logic" and absolute clarity of Leninist "revolutionary legality" (Burbank 1995).

Martens' ability to get the interest of an American company was partially due to his time he spent setting up the Russian Soviet Government Bureau in New York. This Bureau was to act as an informal embassy in the United States, as an instance of exactly this iron logic. Soviet Russia was widely seen as a pariah state that had executed its monarch, defaulted on its previous government's debt obligations, and acted internationally in a charismatic time of expectation of world revolution. Very few states diplomatically recognized the Soviet Union before 1934. In 1919–21, the Russian Soviet Government Bureau was concerned with establishing trade links with the United States, and potentially with diplomatic relations. But important as trade links and recognition were, in the United States, the Bureau saw its chief mission as liaising with and strengthening American Communists. The Bureau ended up treating this foreign territory as part of the Soviet "jurisdiction," where trade and diplomacy were in the end "foolish objectives," and only "the spread of proletarian revolution mattered" (Draper 2003: 162). This "jurisdiction" is the future; that is, it is potentially the Soviet territory in view of imminent changes in the whole world, the World Communist Revolution. But the revolutionary legality of this is seen in a different way by the United States. The New York Police raided the Bureau in 1919. It became the subject of hearings by the US Senate. In 1921, Martens was deported (Raihberg and Shapik 1966).

It was in this context that Martens met Julius Hammer, Communist-minded American businessman, an immigrant from Odessa, and his son Armand. As

Martens was leaving New York, he invited a group of American businessmen to Russia. This group included Armand Hammer. In Moscow, Martens invited Hammer to the Urals, and when Hammer saw the light and offered the supply of grain, Martens recommended Hammer's plan to Lenin. These events show not merely a sequence of *befores* and *afters* that take the narrative of exchanges between Hammer and Soviet government back several years. They also condense relations that were at the same time diplomatic and personal, driven by communist ideas and business interests, and in doing so they complicated the relations of exchange in which Hammer's gifts were part. These relations were fundamentally temporary, but constitutive both of new Soviet order and of different temporalities.

First, these business deals and diplomacy are temporary because the world revolution was forthcoming, whereupon the whole of humanity could join Russia in "being as gods," as the motto of Hammer's gift, *Eritis sicut deus*, put this. Draper argues that this disregard of diplomacy, which seems paradoxical if one of the goals of this mission was the establishment of diplomatic relations, makes sense in a particular temporal orientation of Martens and his colleagues. If World Revolution happens, there is no need for diplomacy and trade; if it does not, diplomacy and trade would not help the Russian Revolution to survive (Draper 2003: 162–63). This also explains the ease with which the Soviet government traded art from the Hermitage and other Russian collections. As Commissar of Foreign Trade Anostas Mokoyan told Hammer in 1928, "we need the money"; he also added jokingly that, "of course one day you have a revolution in your country, and we'll take pictures back, so we are really only lending them to you" (Walker 1974: 236).

Second, they are temporary because they are responses to emergency situations—such as hunger and general post–Civil War devastation and chaos. Third, they are also temporary, as they are themselves in flux of historical change. They make new time, including important changes to the notion of "Soviet new time"— Soviet modernity as time. Between the establishment of the Russian Soviet Government Bureau in 1919, Marten's deportation in 1921, and Hammer's visit to Russia the same year, the ideology of world revolution gave way to ideas about building communism "in a separate country." The internal version of World Revolution was War Communism. This was a radical way to exercise noncapitalism through the state by nationalization of industrial enterprises and banks, including the confiscation of private accounts, tax-like requisition of agricultural "surplus" (that is, everything that exceeded a bare minimum) from peasants for redistribution among the rest of the population, labor duty imposed on "nonlaboring classes," and other attempts at the introduction of nonmonetary economy. War Communism, however, stumbled during the Civil War over the issue of requisition of agricultural surplus, which led to a change of this policy. But this did not prevent peasant rebellions at the end of the Civil War and if not more serious mutiny of Baltic Navy sailors in Kronstadt (1921). Lenin, a master of tactics, quickly substituted the radical assault on capitalism, which he advocated in *The state and revolution* (1917), with gradualism of the "New Economic Policies" (NEP) and temporary tolerance of "elements" of capitalism, including Western concessions (Gillette 1981).

This turn was in Lenin's famous words, "serious and for a long time [*vseriez i nadolgo*]," although he equally famously complicated this temporality by adding that this "long time" was "of course not forever" (Lenin 1970c: 311). In his speech at the 10th Party Conference in May 1921, he very interestingly identifies this shift in terms that oppose the long-term Marxist logic to "expedients"—that is, to the temporary as a matter of the short-term—which is the "philistine" trick of the petty bourgeoisie:

> The [new economic] policy is a long-term one and is being adopted in earnest. We must get this well into our heads and remember it, because, owing to the gossip habit, rumors are being spread that we are indulging in a policy of expedients, that is to say, politics in quotation marks—political trickery—and that what is being done is only for the present day. That is not true. We are taking class relationships into account and have our eyes on what the proletariat must do to lead the peasantry in the direction of communism in spite of everything. Of course, we have to retreat; but we must take it very seriously and look at it from the standpoint of class forces. To regard it as a trick is to imitate the philistines, the petty bourgeoisie, who are alive and kicking [and] not only outside the Communist Party. But I would not go along with Comrade Osinsky in his estimate of the period. He said "seriously and for a long time" meant 25 years. I am not that pessimistic; I shall refrain from estimating the period, but I think his figure is a bit too pessimistic. *We shall be lucky to project our policy for some 5 or 10 years, because we usually fail to do so even for 5 weeks.* (Lenin 1970d: 329–30; emphasis added)

Of course, the longevity had proved not to be the case. But between the time of retreat of military communism under these new policies and the renewed "red guard attack on the capital," which started in the late 1920s, different political

options enter Marxist temporality. Gradualism means a revision of the imminence of world revolution, but it entrenches the state of permanent confron-
tation (rather than "peaceful coexistence")—Antonio Gramsci's "hegemony"
as war of attrition between classes and between socialist and capitalist world
camps. Within Soviet Russia, gradualism meant that the dictatorship of pro-
letariat could entertain a possibility of Chayanov's peasant utopia, and then
dismiss it. This maneuvering within the new time includes the "Stalinist turn"—
the declaration that the temporary retreat is over and time has come for another
speed-up of historical time.

Time: Change and exchange

All this *at once* forms a context for Hammer's 1921 trip and for his personal gift
to Lenin, *Eritis sicut deus*. Let me now sum up how this and other gifts—the
surgical equipment worth $60,000, the very "sudden idea" to exchange grain for
valuables and start an asbestos concession—exists simultaneously in different
temporalities.

There is the "new time" of rapid historical changes in Soviet Russia. This is
the turbulent temporality of war and policy turns, in which, as Lenin puts it,
"we shall be lucky to project our policy for some 5 or 10 years, because we usually fail to do so even for 5 weeks." War Communism, World Revolution, New
Economic Policies, let alone the subsequent turns of the 1920s and 1930s—all
these are modalities of the "new," and changing instances of the "new Soviet
order." But each of these turns assumes different temporalities of state socialism
and world socialism, with different goals and different understandings of the
present. The expectation of World Revolution is a different temporality than the
pragmatics of politics and economics of Soviet construction. This line of quick
historical changes is also a line of *change* between them, which similar to what I
described in chapter 2. We see a sequence of truth claims about the state of the
world, the state of future, and the meanings of the present.

These modalities of *new time*—and radical difference between them—are,
however, practically invisible in the modality of the new time that I have discussed earlier in this chapter. That has to do with a singularity of the historic
break from *before* to *after* that the Museum of Lenin's Kremlin Flat articulates.
As I argued, this is historically a much later construct of time when the Kremlin
opens for the public in 1955, part of the Soviet metanarrative temporal self-
identification but also part of Lenin's commemorative time. By then, the Soviet

narrative of early Soviet history is settled so that its different turns—each having its own before and after—figure uncontroversially in the overall transition from before to after that the Museum and Soviet history books make a singularity.

But in the early 1920s, each of those shifts, with its own different temporal configurations, was a contingency that could have easily led to different kinds of subsequent histories. If Lenin thought they were lucky "to project our policy for some 5 or 10 years, because we usually fail to do so even for 5 weeks," the reverse was also possible: something designed to be short-lived could turn out to be a long-term project. The Soviet saying, "there is nothing more permanent than the temporary" is highly illuminating of the social life of the Soviet state, as I have argued elsewhere (Ssorin-Chaikov 2003).

In this chapter, I focused on just one instance of these changes: the emergence of New Economic Policies and Lenin's turn to foreign concessions. In case of Hammer, this change was enabled by exchange between temporalities. These are the temporalities of the gift, the temporalities of the market, and the temporalities of the Soviet state. Exchanges between the gift and market time are exemplified by Hammer's gift of time—that is, his idea of purchasing grain on credit. Exchanges between the state and market time are exemplified by Lenin's offer of the state time—of the help of Soviet security apparatus to cut through the bureaucratic delays—as part of the business offer to Hammer. This control and security apparatus was essential for the state organization in its many domains, and in particular, for the state "seizure of time" (Verdery 1996) from its ordinary citizens. But in this instance, state time becomes itself a resource for market time of such foreign concessions within the Soviet Union. In turn, this state time and the gift time of Hammer's grain offer are exchanged into temporality of Hammer's business. This exchange enables the longer-term temporality of his wealth. It does so regardless of whether we identify the events of these exchanges analytically as the temporality of noncapitalist resourcing of noncapitalist outside of the market that starts up his big money (a version of the "primitive accumulation") or agree with Hammer that this is one of the gifts of humanitarianism that merely "turns out" to have business effects. (Recall that Lenin's offer of help of emergency powers comes in as help to ensure a speedy delivery of Hammer's grain.) There are different temporalities of capital's origin that also exist in relations of exchange with each other.

What does difference in chronology mean for these exchanges? As we have seen, this difference matters for understanding the timing but also the character of reciprocity of Hammer's gift of the *Eritis sicut deus* sculpture. The single meeting version makes it a countergift for Lenin's gift of Revolution; the two meetings makes it a countergift for Lenin's business offer.

This leads to the question of the relations that we see being set up. To what extent are there gift or business relations? Interestingly, it only seems that this difference of interpretation is a matter the Soviet versus American perspectives on these exchanges. As we have seen, Lenin and Martens have no qualms in identifying this exchange as business from the start. For Lenin, this is true from the first meeting with Hammer in October 1921. For Martens, this was so even earlier—from his invitation of Hammer and other US businessmen to visit Russia, which he made as he was expelled from New York. The difference between business and gift perspectives parallels changes that exist between the early 1920s and the subsequent Soviet system. It is this later Soviet order of time that retrospectively fixes the temporary character of NEP by making it into a market means to a nonmarket end.

But in the context of the early 1920s, both business and gift relations constitute and undo the binary divisions of *before* versus *after* as well as the *Soviet society* versus the *capitalist West*. They interlink, make use of, and simultaneously distinguish the temporality of capitalist business, the temporality of gift and the temporality of the emerging Soviet state. And all these are characterized by accelerations in which giving time—the gift of modernity as the gift of new time—is constituted by trying to take as little time as possible. But business and the state, and not gift, have drawn much of research attention here. The gift of time prompts a question of how it can be theorized as a gift in the Soviet context, and not just as time. I address this question in chapter 5.

CHAPTER 4

Time for the field diary

Interlude

Nikolai stepped toward the door of the tent, and stumbled over the dog, Iaponets ("Japanese"). The dog was asleep, and didn't move at all or make any noise. Iaponets! I called it in my thoughts. Clever dog. Nikolai looked at old Nikolai and the girls. Everyone was asleep. What is the time? He felt in his pocket for his wristwatch but it was not there. But there were four pieces of matches of different lengths. One match was for "Mukhachev," another match was for "the boat." What were the other two? He reached for his coat behind his reindeer skin bed and lifted it quietly, feeling the weight of the notebook and the watch. When he turned to the door again, he again stepped on the dog; it murmured something in its sleep but not loudly, and it did not wake up.

Nikolai pulled the tent cover down behind him. It was 7:50 a.m. The morning was grey. Only one log was smoking on the campfire. Overnight the fire has eaten up the much of the three logs, and slowly died in a grey spot of ashes; the remainder of the logs pointed in different directions. More smoke was coming out of the metal stovepipe of the other tent in the camp. The pup that was tied to that tent had stretched his leash and was facing the tent; it gave Nikolai only a quick glance. Lenin's tent was clearly awake. Why do they never fix the campfire if they are up before everyone else? Nikolai lifted the logs one by one, moved them toward the center of the fireplace, and dropped them so that they flapped each other. Only one was barely glimmering, and the fire did not restart. I sat down on one of the logs and took out the notebook. Ok. 1. Mukhachev; 2.

The boat. Yes, Lenin took down the boat from cache [labaz]. *What were the other two? I know what they are. I know what they are. He penciled these two points down, then put the pencil down and looked at a very brief entry from yesterday:*
    April 27 [1994], Wednesday.

1. *thunderstorm in April.*
2. *Dima and Larisa's reaction to Mukhachev (Old Nikolai threatens to set fire to trapper's huts).*
3. *Shamans in 1938.*

The diary's entry actually elaborated these points after this list. This was not always the case. These broken matches served as reminders of conversations, to not forget to write about them. I turned a few pages. They were full of such lists: three or four points to remember, often left as they were, while the diary's narrative turned to something else. "Everyday hierarchies in Evenki forest camp" was a paper title I thought it would be good to write, back in early April. I closed the notebook, put it in my pocket, and walked to Lenin's tent. I pulled the tent cover, smelling dough that Lenin's wife, Nadezhda, was whipping up in a pan to make bread. Lenin and one of his sons, Arsen, were sitting on the other side of the tent with mugs of tea. "Nikolai, come in, have some tea," he said, "I am going to the [geodesic] tower today. Would you like to come along?"

***

James Joyce's *Ulysses* was the only novel I had with me during my fieldwork in Katonga in 1993–95. In the forest, I was traveling light. I had only a backpack that I was prepared to carry myself when I walked to another camp or the village, without the help of reindeer or sleigh. In writing my field diary, as in the opening paragraphs above, a couple of times I tried to imitate Joyce's style, mixing third- and first-person narrative. In this particular instance, I did not go much further. The notes that I took that morning were prompted by a matchstick that I had snapped and stored in my pocket as a reminder to later write down "topic 1": "Lenin: no camp fire." I wanted to remember to think about why Vladimir's tent never fixed the campfire if they were up before me and my camp companions (old Nikolai and his granddaughters). I used matches to generate such reminders for myself, as the ethnographic notebook was a killer of ethnographic conversations. I had on countless occasions learned this the hard way—my field notes for one episode indicate this text: "When I took the notebook out, Dima stumbled in the middle of the sentence, and said, 'Why? Write this down later'"; "The notebook killed the conversation again"; "Why did I try to write this down as an interview? When will it be now that we come to this topic?" In the forest, I did not use a voice recorder most of the time as forest camps have no electricity, and I could not carry around the sufficient supply of batteries. But the social effect of voice recorder was even more disruptive when I taped quite a large corpus of interviews in the village.

This was despite the fact that people knew from the start that I was there "to write things down about Evenki life." They did not object to this, and virtually no one refused to talk to me, or to have me around. I was explicit that I was interested in the present as well as in the recent Soviet past, rather than the traditional culture, a research concern of Soviet-style ethnography with which Evenki were quite familiar. The difference took some time to explain, but eventually it was accepted. However, my explanations always lagged behind their decision to have an anthropologist around. The temporality of explanations is different from temporality of decisions; research consent is not a matter of appointment but of complex givens—of temporalities that are established through the histories of anthropological presence. Permission or nonpermission was most of the time given to me before I had a chance to thoroughly explain my reasons. When I first came to Katonga in the summer of 1989, I went to the forest with hunters and reindeer herders who came to the village to buy supplies. People who did not want to take me back with them simply pretended they did not hear or understand my request when I approached them. The first person that did agree did so also immediately: "Excellent! You will tell us all about Moscow, and if you have met Gorbachev."

I travelled with him to his forest camp where I was passed to another host, an elder who was a decorated World War II veteran and a respected reindeer herder, and whose name was, like mine, Nikolai. When he agreed to host me, it also happened faster than I could anticipate or explain. Before offering tea, he said, "drop your things over there, this will be your bed." Then he put my presence in terms of the obligations to help ethnographers as those who themselves partake in "the help that the state provides to the small peoples of the North" (*pomosch gosudarstva malym narodam severa*). In saying this to me, he gave me back the narrative of ethnography as an instrument of twentieth-century developmental time (see chapter 2). In 1989, he told me, "you are here to ask, and we have an obligation [*obiazanost'*] to answer"; he repeated that in 1994. But this too preceded whatever I had to say about the purposes of my visit. The tempo of his reply had instantly made me feel obligated (cf. Bourdieu 1991), despite the fact that this was put in terms of Evenki obligations in response to the Soviet and Russian gift of modernity. This quick act masterfully produced relations of hospitality out of a responsible response to a call of research duty, if we think about this in Soviet terms, or a contractual agreement of sorts envisioned by Human Subject Protocols, if we think about this in terms of social science research in the United States.

Yet there was an irony to this mastery. As I quickly learned, to agree to have an ethnographer around is not the same thing as having time to answer this ethnographer's questions. A match in my pocket, broken for a topic to remember, was about that too. Vladimir "Lenin" was among the people who welcomed and hosted me from the start, but he also exemplified the temporal complexity of my research exchanges. We did talk a lot, but most of the time those conversations took place at the time of his own choosing: "I wanted to rest and read, but Vladimir wants to talk," I recorded a few times. At times, Vladimir and other Evenki felt compelled to tell a long story, and have a long conversation. But more often, the reply to my questions would be simply, "*tymanne*," which is Evenki for "tomorrow."

Chronotope

In the present chapter, I approach my field diary as a *chronotope* (Bakhtin 1975). As a diary, it is structured by dates, by repetitions and elaborations of themes and structures. It is "full of . . . lists of three and four points" that could nonetheless be paths that lead astray: "points to remember that are often left as they were, while the diary's narrative turned to something else." Apart from the multiple temporalities of the present and such incomplete memories, it is full of incomplete futures: "'Everyday hierarchies in Evenki forest camp' was a paper title I thought it would be good to write, back in early April." But when I had it out, this notebook marked the presence of the state. Vladimir "Lenin" and old Nikolai were aware that Evenki, like other Siberian indigenous peoples, were systematically studied, and that the state had accumulated considerable archives on them that included substantial ethnographic materials. Whether I wanted it or not, it was the state time of the field notebook time that made my interlocutors uncomfortable talking during formal interviews, and that shaped both the form and the content of the on-the-record conversations. My conversations with my Evenki interlocutors froze in a way that was familiar to me from the moment I saw how Evenki talked to the collective farm director (chapter 2). At that moment, I as ethnographer was interpolating my interlocutors into being state subjects—and I was myself interpolated as one. This in turn affected the internal temporality of my field note writing. But my notebook also acted as a material object in the temporality of its external ethnographic context. This agency of writing, on the one hand, underscores *construction* of a research fact (Latour and Woolgar 1986)—abbreviations, edits, and memories that underscore whatever I later take as a description. On the other hand, it reveals "relationships of power and histories of encounter," which "make anthropology itself already a part of . . . subjects of study" (Marcus and Myers 1995: 2). Diary as a narrative and as material artifact makes time, to use the Mikhail Bakhtin's words, "palpable and visible" while space is "intensified and sucked into the movement of time, plot, history" (Bakhtin 1975: 235), and, we can add, an anthropological argument. The argument in this chapter is that this notebook marks the state in a form of time, and that the state time exists in complex relations of exchange with research time.

I will elaborate on this by looking at the time I was given "to ask questions," at when I was able to have my notebook out and write, and what this writing meant in terms of microsocial space around me. I will explore these temporalities of my presence among Evenki and the temporalities of my notebook as inscribing the presence of the state. I will do so from the point of view that research (ethnography) is itself time rather than something that simply happens *in* time, to borrow Nancy Munn's formulation (1983: 280). But by adding research time to the multiple temporalities that I explore in this book, I do not assume that it is as another "one" among "many" that I explore. To be sure, research time is composite, as there are different discrete temporalities of conversations and interactions, and an enduring time of participation in everyday life. There is institutional time of the academy, including funding time and writing time in and after research. But ethnography is also a Bergsonian duration, in which the flow of experiences and records, while rooted in long-term fieldwork, spans beyond individual fieldwork locations and is continuous across projects. In this chapter, I focus on the relationship between research time and state time by linking two kinds of materials. The first materials are my ethnographic notes and experiences in Siberia, which I have already introduced; the second materials, to be explored in the second part of this chapter, are research materials associated with an exhibition of gifts to Soviet leaders, which art historian Olga

Sosnina and I curated in Moscow in 2006 and where the *Eritis sicut deus* figurine that Lenin-the-Soviet-leader received from Armand Hammer was shown, along with more than 500 other gifts.

The reason I will move to this second project later in this chapter is that I turned to thinking about the temporality of my Siberian ethnography only *after* I moved on to the gifts to Soviet leaders. From this point of view, even the account of my first fieldwork in Katonga in 1989 that I outlined above is not a "live" recording of arrival but a retrospection in which the second project also has a presence. But if in my Siberian ethnography the time of my notebook was an instance of the Soviet state and its legacies in the 1990s, then the project on gifts to Soviet leaders and its research archive became an instance of the postsocialist state in the making: in the ways in which this project blurred in radical ways the distinction between research time and the time of public presentation of research results as well as between this project's academic, popular, and state audience, and between the relations that this research time described, performed, and created.

In the conclusion of his famous essay, "The time and the chronotope of the modern novel," Mikhail Bakhtin observes that fiction's textual chronotope— "the chronotope of the depicted world"—extends beyond text and enters the worlds of these depictions' author, performer, listener, and reader, and that "these worlds are also chronotopic." It is there that he acknowledges that chronotopes are multiple. Each "major chronotope" may contain an unlimited number of "minor" ones, to the point that each motif is a chronotope of its own kind. In my case, this would be the motif of a broken match, a marker of memory, held in unsteady place to be retrieved, *maybe*, into narrative, later. Chronotopes may include each other, coexist, and be interwoven so that their interlocking is outside a given single chronotope (Bakhtin 1975: 400–401). In this chapter, I ask what changes if the concept of chronotope is applied, not to literature, but research? What if Bakhtin's author is not a writer but a scholar? In this case, what would be "the chronotope of the depicted world," and what are the chronotopic relations of this depicted world with "these depictions' author, performer, listener, and reader"?

Slowness

The flip side of ethnography as a Bergsonian duration is what George Marcus (2003) describes as the "unbearable slowness of being an anthropologist now."

He draws attention to duration as having speed, and refers to a chronic belatedness of ethnography in relation to the pace of changes in societies that we study. In turn, Paul Rabinow's anthropology of the contemporary makes a research tool out this problem. Chronic belatedness makes ethnography a chronicle of "what is taking place without deducing it beforehand"; furthermore, this is an "accompaniment" of a particular time when "no single sensibility—modernist or otherwise—dominates, overarches, or underlies current affairs" (Rabinow 2008: 3, 78; Rabinow 2011). The argument is that changes can no longer be framed in terms of teleology of transitions: from modernity to postmodernity or from state socialism to neoliberalism. As Tobias Rees puts this, "By turning toward the study of the 'here and now'—rather than of the 'far-away' and 'timeless'—anthropologists experience profound temporal turbulences precisely because they can no longer make assumptions about what is necessary for their method to produce rich ethnographic data—a temporally stable scene and subject of study" (Rees 2008: 7).

The previous state of affairs—the "temporally stable scene and subject of study"—as research temporality has been constituted by the overlap of the Western calendar year that organizes the academic graduate or sabbatical fieldwork (a year *at least* in the field), and the conceptual construction of societal or cultural reproduction cycles in societies that are being explored. What comes under question now is precisely this temporality of reproduction. An assumption of cyclical time that is thought to dominate "traditional" societies under study is contrasted with linear time of Western society and anthropology that include their own cyclicality, but of a "geometrical" sort (Leach 1961: 126) that neatly adds up to a chronological linear. Cultural differences are then highlighted through the incongruence of this geometry of Western temporal vision of cyclicality versus the fluidity of social rhythms under study.

The anthropology of the contemporary is marked by a double departure from this vision. First, it is a departure of anthropology from non-Western or traditional societies to modernity that is characterized by such geometrical time. Second, it is a departure of modernity itself from this geometrical time to "flexible" timescapes (see, for example, Adam 1998; Harvey 1989). Global flows of persons, things, technologies, and ideas challenge not just fieldwork conditions but the very constitution of the field itself as a location (Gupta and Ferguson 1997a, 1997b; Marcus 1995) and time (Dalsgaard and Nielsen 2013) that consistently resists geometrical spatial and temporal scales. Anthropology's coming "home" from the study of "far-way" and "timeless" (Rees 2008) happens to coincide with modernity's line of flight ("modernity at large," see Appadurai 1996) into various forms of the contemporary.

One question about this transformation is this: if the point of departure is marked by the assumptions of "traditional" cyclical time versus "modern" linear time, this move itself is not contingent on the assumption of linear time. This double transformation is easily described as a shift, a "time's arrow" (Hodges 2008), or the "straight time" (Boellstorff 2007). But even if this transformation could be described in terms of a liner vector, does it mean that the time of this transformation is singular? If we arrive at a temporality that resists geometry, is this temporality applicable to the temporality of this transformation?

If, however, this temporality in not singular, then what exactly is the "unbearable slowness" of anthropology? Belatedness pervades any kind of fieldwork—given the waiting time for a good moment to ask (which is so often a failure), of the sense of being late to ask and to see, and to fail to remember what one has seen and asked about, when finally having time to write this down. What exactly is speed and slowness here? We can think of this in terms of the paradox of speed: if we move in the same speed with the objects that we study this is actually, by a physical frame-of-reference definition, *stillness*. It is, then, only a relative slowness that allows us to see the speed of anything. Let me think through this slowness below, where I slow down ethnographically to a single day—April 28, 1994—but then approach this day as a chronotope of research time that spans forward to the present (to my more contemporary research and the present time of writing this book) and across some different temporalities that I chart. In doing so, I take inspiration from Joyce's description of a single day and Alexander Sokurov's camera gaze in his *Russian ark*, a film that depicts the history of the Hermitage Museum in a hour-and-a-half-long single shot. But before I do that, let me introduce the time of the ethnographic notebook a little bit more.

Time of the notebook (i)

A day in the forest camp has its own routine cyclicality, which changes throughout the year; seasonal variation and weather can make a lot of difference. When I was in the forest camp, people did not wake up very early, or very quickly. But once a fire had been set in a tent's stove, roughly between 7 a.m. and 8 a.m.—by the wife of the tent's head (*bye*, the tent's "man") if he had one, or by whomever was up first—its warmth served as a signal to all to get out of bed. After a quick tea, preparations were made for the day's work. If there were travel plans, like Vladimir's plans that morning, reindeer had to be caught, saddled, or harnessed. This might take some time, as the reindeer herd could be far from the camp, even if they are attracted to camp by smokes that are set to drive away the mosquitos in summer, or attracted by salt in winter. If setting the camp smoke as well as the tent fire marks the beginning of the day, catching reindeer and the second tea midmorning, which is the main meal that all tent inhabitants have at the same time, marks the beginning of the work (*rabochii den'*, "work day"). This work day is a translation of social rhythms of the forest camps into the time of collective farms and urban Russia—that is, into temporalities that are based on the divisions of work and leisure, and work time and home time. In Evenki, to work (*khavaldiami*) is to do everything except for eating and sleeping, from cooking at home to hunting and reindeer herding.

Although I occupied a recognized role of someone who is there "to ask questions," it was expected that I to take part in the day's work to the best of my abilities. This involved no hunting in my case; instead, I was tasked with some reindeer herding (like rounding up reindeer when they are needed to be brought to the camp), and lots of fetching firewood and water, sawing and cutting logs for the tent stove, and participating in the construction of reindeer fences (which is important seasonal work in spring and late summer) or their frequent inspection. During the day in the camp, people are busy or simply gone, and have no time for conversations. If I stayed in the camp after the second tea time, I was left in one part of the gendered forest chronotope: women were left behind in the camp, and had to find time for my questions in the middle of bread baking, laundry, making clothes or winter boots, etc. When I was gone with men, I was in the other part of this chronotope. But it was during that work time in the camp or in the forest that I developed my arts of memory, with the system of reminders by matches that I broke differently as markers of different topics. The best conversations I had were during work breaks for tea or smoking, for instance, during the construction of reindeer fences, which was done by the adult men of the camp. On these occasions, all men were at ease, throwing questions back and forth, and talking at the same time. In contrast, during evening time, when we were back at camp and most of day's work was done, the social space centered on the figure of the male head of the household. In this evening time, I found it difficult in the tent to ask anyone else but him, or invite someone else out for a conversation. During this time, when I did what I was supposed to do as ethnographer—that is, "to ask"—I resumed this head-centered social space in a slightly ritualized role of the guest, with my questions and, this time, a notebook out. This is a crossing point of daily temporalities of gender and age authority, and that of the state, as represented here by my presence and my notebook.

Jean Briggs, in her celebrated book on Inuit social and emotional landscapes, speaks of "a tent of one's own" as a place of reflection and retreat where she could give in to her own emotions among people who were "never in anger" (Briggs 1970). During my fieldwork in the forest, I did not have such a tent of my own. I shared a tent with my hosts, staying in the back, right of the tent's entry and its stove. The left side belonging to the tent's head and was his family space. This was a crowded space, but the social skills with which people interacted—comparable with the scenario that Briggs describes—never made me feel like this space cramped. I frequently thought these *taiga* Evenki would make ideal spaceship crews. But it was my fieldwork notebook that marked my private space as private time. When I had it out not to ask questions but to write, this was a sign that I don't want any conversations, questions, or jokes.

The time of the notebook was for me a way to fence myself off. In this form, the notebook had the capacity of an agent not merely to mark my identity as an outsider but also to mark my presence as an instance of a state time. This state time had daily fluctuations. When I was fetching firewood, or rounding the reindeer, or cutting larches for a reindeer fence that we dashed through the thickets and glades of *taiga*, I was not completely outside this state time, but the state time itself morphed into work time. In other words, the time that was initially given to me as ethnographer as an obligation and in return for modernity as new time (see chapter 5) is then itself changed into something different. Clifford Geertz (1973), in his ethnography of the Balinese cockfight, describes how the ice was broken between him and the participants in this illegal activity when they together ran away from the police. During my own fieldwork, I had many similar moments of solidarity with my interlocutors through similar complicity. But the state time of my presence had a capacity of being dissolved in ways that were similar to this as well as being reestablished. State time resumed as such when I had my notebook out in the evening, or even when I asked a question—for example, during a break in fence construction: "But you are supposed to be paid for this work by the collective farm, aren't you?" However informal our conversation could be before this question, it would have a strong interpolating affect.

In 1988 and 1989, my trips were official research trips from the Institute of Ethnography, Russian Academy of Sciences, with travel documents that needed to be stamped in local soviets that had a duty to accommodate the researcher and help to set up the project. But I did not need these state travel documents to go to the forest, and I left them behind in the village. In 1993, when I returned to Katonga, I did so not as a researcher from Moscow but as a PhD student from Stanford University. This time I did not have Russian state documents with me, but I also did not need them in the new post-Soviet context. The state route in was still important (and remains so today) for archival work, where access is given on the basis of institutional support letters. But while these documents marked my entry into the field, their necessity as artifacts remained stored away at the gates of this project. By the time I left Katonga in 1989, forest Evenki introduced me to others as someone who "nomadized with them" (*kocheval s nami*). This joint experience marked my ethnographic identity through a different notion of time—despite the fact that my notebook continued to be an instance of the Russian state time in the late 1980s and even during subsequent work in 1993–95. Even then, from Vladimir's and old Nikolai's point of view I was there on "business of state importance" (*delo gosudarstvennoi vazhnosti*), despite that I was institutionally an American anthropologist.

Nails

Vladimir and his tent joined with us two days ago to continue something they started earlier: building a boat. They were working on it over the last two years; the wood for it needed to dry on a cache (*dylkon*) they had in this area. Vladimir already spotted a good aspen for this boat a few years back, and he planned his late spring camps in this area so that he could work on the boat. The day before, I saw them taking down this boat's base—very skillfully dug from this aspen trunk—from the cache.

After he arrived, Vladimir explained that he saw such boats being made when he was very young, "after the war" (World War II), but since that time they were not built. From the late 1960s onward, it was possible to borrow inflatable rubber boats in the collective farm or purchase them the village shop. But in post-Soviet years Vladimir could not afford such a boat, and he decided to build one. And this was no birch-bark canoe (*berestianka*) that Evenki built until the early 1950s, but a modified dugout that Vladimir saw made by Finnish exiles from Karelia that, together with the Germans, were brought to Katonga during the war. "They were brought here on a barge they have hauled up the river, and just dumped there for the winter, together with the barges but with no food." A lot of them died, but some were adopted by Evenki and lived in this area until the mid-1950s; it was then that young Vladimir saw their boat-making skills.

Building such a boat was a gamble, as Vladimir and his son, Arsen, did not have much experience in doing this. But this was a necessary gamble—new market prices for such commodities as boats had risen sharply after 1991, in the conditions of a considerable demonetization of the economy. This gamble had its own temporality, as they needed to dry the wood to make planks, and they knew that a year for this task would probably be not enough. And then there were a number of problems that appeared over the course of construction that they had not considered from the start. One of these issues was that they did not have tar to caulk the boat once it was assembled. Arsen suggested using pine resin to make tar, and this seemed like a good idea. Another issue, and a more immediate difficulty, was that they needed nails to make the boat's top into a solid frame that would hold it together. When I came to Vladimir's tent one morning, which I described at the beginning of this chapter, I caught the end of discussion on this issue. The previous day, they failed to fix the frame with ropes that they had made from reindeer skin. Vladimir thought of an old geodesic tower, erected not far from the camp in the 1970s. It was made of wood, and we could get some nails from it. He offered the opportunity for me to accompany him.

That morning, after a reindeer was caught and saddled, Vladimir and I set off for this tower. Vladimir rode his reindeer, and I walked behind him. It was late spring, and we took a reindeer sleigh route that was a beaten track that was ice-solid underground but covered by water from melting snow. But at least it was not as soggy as everything else this time of year. It took us about two hours to get to the tower, and during the few stops that we made, Vladimir told me about how he took part in building such towers in the 1970s, working with geodesists who demarcated the forest space with these towers and detailed maps. Geodesists hired collective farm reindeer and Evenki guides to take them around. He told me how he preferred this work to reindeer herding. "I am a *modern* Evenki" (*Ia—sovremennyi Evenk*). This was not the first time he said this. In the evening, when I wrote this down, I went through my notebook looking at other occasions when he repeated this locution. These include the times when he told me that he visited Moscow in the late 1960s, when he told me that he liked to study, and also a day before our trip when he and Arsen took down the boat. "We are modern Evenki," he explained at that time, "because we look for opportunities that modern life brings us." He referred to the skill of making Finnish boats, which counted as modern despite he observed this boat making "after the war."

We approached the tower. We saw that the construction included a shed at its bottom—a half-ruined foundation under a roof. It was in the inner side of the roof that we found nails that were not rusted and therefore could be used. But there was a problem, as we had only axes and no pliers to take them out. Axes and knives are the main tools that Vladimir and other Evenki have in the forest. They use axes very skillfully to make practically everything they need, and that was the main tool to manufacture the boat base and the planks. But now when we tried to split the wood to take the nails out, we failed; the roof was reinforced with iron staples that we needed to take out, too. We struggled for some time and realized that the only way we could get to the nails was if we were to burn the shed. We managed to break the shed's roof off the tower, set the fire, and put the roof in. Then we had some time to wait until it was burned enough so that we could get the nails. By the fire, Vladimir continued to tell me about his memories of work with the geodesists until we both paused at a thought that crossed our minds simultaneously. The tower is still operational. Is it legal to take part of it down? "Nikolai," asked Vladimir, "will you write down that this is just a shed [we are burning down], and not the tower?" "Sure," I replied, "and, besides, I did this together with you."

If my notebook was a state artifact in the forest, it was not the only state artifact around. Geodesic towers, just as the combined fodder (see chapter 2), were part of the state infrastructure that marked the state as modernity and development. These, together with abandoned oil exploration derricks east of this area as well as old trading bases and storages of leftover fuel, became a resource—almost an object of subsistence gathering, utilized often in an unexpected ways. The topography of this Soviet debris (Ssorin-Chaikov 2016)—of these projects of modernity-as-time that were ruined and lived as a "second hand time," to use a formulation from the novel by Svetlana Alexievich (2013)—had a particular temporality of memory. One needed to remember where these things were, and what they were. Arsen's knowledge in this regard did not entirely overlap with Vladimir's knowledge; the latter traveled extensively with geodesists and geologists as a "modern Evenki." Vladimir knowledge also included memories of how exiled Finns had survived, and how they built dugouts. In other parts of Siberia, these were memories of gulag barracks that were used to enlarge indigenous settlements and collective farms (Ulturgasheva 2012). This memory was complex and often ambiguous in relation to identity, but the leftovers of their presence added to the state landscape that now could be utilized. Thus, it was not just a narrative of the past but also a resource in the uncertain present and the even more uncertain future.

If the temporality of daily rhythms, seasonal migrations, and trade is cyclical, like coming to the same area in spring to continue working on the boat, this secondhand time of state infrastructure is that of memory of singular past events. For example, Vladimir recalled his trips with geodesists that were regular but had a finality of the work that needed to be done only once, that now enabled our trip to get the nails from the shed, which we could burn only once—and which was in effect a minor metonym for the transformative event of the end of the Soviet era as our initial worry of wrongdoing quickly changed into indifference: the state that erected this tower was no longer there to look after it. But as a result of the long-term temporality of my fieldwork, I came to realize that the contrast between the cyclical time of Evenki ecology and economy and the event-time of transformations (Badiou 2005) was not necessarily the best way to describe what was taking place. This contrast is not useful because both are complex assemblages of repetition and difference (Deleuze 2004). Cyclicality was each time improvised to a great degree: knowledge of good pastures and hunting grounds is similarly a chronotope of the events of past travel, while event-time of engagement with the state infrastructure was based on a number of practical and narrative repetitions. Vladimir told me many times that to do things such as making a dugout boat and fetch nails from Soviet-era tower was "to live like our grand-dads" (Rus. *po dedovski*), like "before" (Ev. *amaski*)—that is, to be self-reliant. This was in no contradiction, in his eyes, to telling me on other occasions that taking advantage of these ruins was a marker of being "modern Evenki." It is also clearly possible to describe this improvisation of Finnish boat building in actor-network terms of agency (Callon 1986) of axes and fire, which is not merely a symmetrical network space of people and objects but also a temporality of the already existing materiality. Axe-as-a-tool leads to fire-as-a-tool to produce nails. For Vladimir, this is both "modern" and "grand-dads" because it is making use of circumstances that are not fixed by an endpoint event—by the fact of whether the boat was made in the end or not. Ironically, while this is quite far from the contexts that Rabinow had in mind when he formulated the agenda for the anthropology of the contemporary (Rabinow 2008), it is precisely the temporality that he envisions: of "now" without the completion.

Lenin

We have just finished the soup. A few pieces of moose meat are still out on the wooden tray on the tent's floor, and our bowls still have some broth with macaroni. "Well," says Vladimir, taking out his knife and cleaning the tray into a empty soup pan, "this is for the dogs." Arsen, my tent companion (nicknamed Churchill), and I pass our bowls to Nadezhda. There is a disappointment in the air as this is a good time for a smoke, but we were out of the village for too long, and cigarettes are over. In the form of these commodities, modernity is time too, and not just new time but also the time of supplies that run out. The notebook is an interesting product of a similar situation, that is, of me running out of the batteries for the voice recorder. As is the case with Vladimir's skills, the notebook (and its state time) is both "modern" and "grand-dads." I clean my hands with a towel, which I then stick behind the tent's pole, and take my notebook out. While I do this, Vladimir produces a pack of cigarettes from behind his bed. "Emergency supplies [*neprikosnovennyi zapas*]," he laughs and passes them around. "I was telling you," he turns to me, "we used to travel much more. I studied in Igarka [town in the north of Krasnoyarsk province], and this was on a Komsomol travel ticket [*komsomol'skaia putevka*]." I am reminded that on other occasions he told me that on such an order of Komsomol travel ticket he was sent to Moscow in 1967. This is when he visited the Kremlin, and the Lenin Museum. Vladimir and others finish smoking and make it clear they are going to bed. It was a long day. Churchill and I walk back to old Nikolai's tent, where he prepares two of his granddaughters to sleep, although this is normally Churchill's duty while their parents are away.

"Did you have tea at Vladimir's?" asks old Nikolai. I nod. "Did you ask him questions [*rassprashival*]?" "Yes," I reply, "about his time as a student." Old Nikolai is always uneasy that in the forest camp it is not only of him that I ask questions. It is fine if I spend the day with Vladimir obtaining the nails for the boat. It is less fine if I have an evening meal in his tent after we return. But in this competitive ownership over the daily time of an anthropologist, it is more or less fine if I inquire about Vladimir's personal and biographical details, while old Nikolai wants to be the sole authority on "the Evenki old ways" (*raneshneie*). This is another construction of the anthropological time. If he recognizes that my presence in the forest is a "business of state importance," and if he is to fulfill his obligation to answer, it should be only *he* who is called to this duty. "Yes," he goes on, "everybody knows this story. I have told you when he came back [from Moscow], we were laughing: 'To study, to study, and to study,'" he imitates

Vladimir imitating Lenin after this trip to Moscow. (The phrase originates in Lenin's 1923 articles in the newspaper, *Pravda*: "Our task in the renewal of our state apparatus is, first, to study, second, to study, and, third, to study, and then to check that our science does not become a dead letter or a fashionable word [as it often does, let us confess], but really came into out flesh and blood and became an element in our composition" [Lenin 1970b: 391]). The triple slogan "to study, to study, and to study" became a Soviet cliché, and was repeated on posters and in schools from Moscow to the Evenki District. Old Nikolai imitated Vladimir quoting these words, including an attempt at Vladimir's voice and hand gestures: "Words, hammered in copper [*chekannye med'iu slova*]." Old Nikolai says this solemnly. "You know," he adds, "this was so funny we called Vladimir as 'Lenin' ever since: 'To teach, to teach, and to teach.' What was it [Lenin's phrase], 'to teach' [*uchit'*] or 'to study' [*uchitsia*], Nikolai?"

Churchill laughed, and I did as well, although old Nikolai had indeed told me this story several times already. Vladimir's nickname was "Lenin," because his wife was called Nadezhda, because of a characteristic hand gesticulation that was reminiscent of Lenin (or at least of his image in Soviet movies), and also because of this Moscow trip. Such conversations are fragments of these narratives, which I found, however, never told as whole stories. These are half-told and even part-told stories, where the whole is given by abbreviation. The whole point of Vladimir's story was, for example, that "we *used* to travel much more." This was a commentary on travels of the past that are no longer possible. By this he was not referring to forest nomadism or even his work with geodesists but to travel outside the collective farm and the district that was made possible by Soviet reforms. The travel he referred to was a matter of Soviet distributive economy (Verdery 1991)—for instance, Young Communist (Komsomol) "travel tickets" that were organizational recruitment, which was a form of order; or quotas for "young pioneer camps" for holidays in the south of Krasnoyarsk province where quite a number of Katonga Evenki recalled going in the 1970s or his trip to Moscow.

There were the gifts of modernity that opened up the Soviet space for travel and career possibilities, real for some and imagined for all. This was a story of Soviet development that from this Siberian perspective seemed to be an endless, if not global space. But in 1994, the point of this story was a rapid and forceful contraction of this space. This was the story not of the old ways but the new emplacement of these Evenki at the time of "wild capitalism" of the 1990s, when Russia quickly integrated into the global market and became one of the sites of import of a global commodity of the gift of development: the neoliberal reforms. In the course of these changes, outside travel became a commodified space well beyond the reach of these collective-farm herders and hunters. On mass, people stopped traveling far, and not just to Krasnoyarsk but also to regional centers like Tura and Baikit. Local seasonal travel of school children from boarding school to forest camps became slow; it was no longer done in less then an hour by helicopter but instead in two or three days by reindeer. While new configurations of post-Soviet economy channel new commodities across the post-Soviet space, and while these included in northern Siberia not just consumables, clothes, and hunting and fishing equipment, but also tourist possibilities, the very same market flows created new barriers and new bounded localities. This space as an "anthropological location" (Gupta and Ferguson 1997a) is simultaneously, and in very differentiating ways, unbound and bounded (cf. Rogers 2010).

The socialist realism of memory

> Thank you for the Exhibition. Today I visited my happy childhood. I do not want to leave but keep watching and watching, and recall all that was good under the Soviet power.
>
> . . .
>
> Once I walked out of the museum to the street, I became very sad, very sad that this all does not exist any more. Only now I understand that what is most important in life is not money but relations between human beings. (Visitors' book, *Gifts to Soviet leaders*; Ssorin-Chaikov 2006b)

In the 1990s, I thought about my Siberian research material primarily through the lens of paradoxes of globalization. I approached new territorialization and new subsistence economies as the flip side of the opening of the former Soviet space. The neoliberal logic of global political economy became opportunity for some and crisis for others (cf. Ssorin-Chaikov 2003). My newer research on gift giving to Soviet leaders, and particularly the 2006 exhibition of these gifts, gave me another angle to look at the same material.

Gifts to Soviet leaders is a project that looks at the vast and complex economy of official gifts that the heads of the Soviet Union attracted from Soviet subjects and international readers and movements. These gifts ranged from military uniforms from Red Army units, china from porcelain factories, and towels from peasant women, to industrial artifacts such as models of nuclear missiles and pieces of Trans-Siberian railroad. This kind of gifting was as important as a way to navigate Soviet identities and ideologies, as were other forms of noncommodified exchange in socialist "redistributive economies." Research into these practices of exchange was to be my next long-term project. But it was a product of a very differently structured research time, and it created a very different research archive. I started it when I moved to a full-time university job. I carried it out not as long-term participant observation but through a series of relatively short research intervals during breaks in the academic year. I started to publish on it and cocurated an exhibition before I had research completed.

Furthermore, this project is itself not one research but two projects. Because of the resonance these publications and the exhibition held in Russia, I extended it from the Soviet past to the post-Soviet present, focusing on reactions to it as a form of cultural memory, post-Soviet identity politics, and a modality of relations between museums and the state. In this context, the exhibition became a research tool, and its book of visitors' comments became a public ethnographic notebook of this project.

It is interesting that if this exhibition was about what was given to the leaders—and it included Hammer's gift of the sculpture, *Eritis sicut deus*—many responses were about what they *received* from the state. Comments of the exhibition visitors have drawn my attention to the idiom of gift in narratives of loss. This idiom is similar in these otherwise very different contexts. In Katonga, many of my informants, including old Nikolai and Vladimir "Lenin," talked of career, work, and travel opportunities, and also "help" (*pomosch*) and "development" (*razvitie*) as something *given* to them in the past. Exhibition visitors remarked that in Soviet times "the state gave us the opportunity to implement Lenin's slogan, 'Study, study and, one more time, study,'" while "now education and healthcare are not free." "The Soviet times were the fairest in the social respect"; "people started *receiving* jobs," while "now there is unemployment in the country"; and "we *received* free education," "we *received* stipends and free lunches" (emphasis added):

> I am 76 years old. Before the Revolution, my grandfather was a street cleaner, and my grandmother was a laundress. My mother was a bookkeeper. [But] I had a long and fulfilling life. I am a second generation Leningrader. [I lived through the] Leningrad blockade [of the Second World War], was wounded, and evacuated to Kuban'.

The Exhibition has shown all that the Soviet power gave to my generation. I started my working life at the age of 14, and finished at 60 when I retired. I have two higher education degrees, and I received both without leaving production work. I started my career as a plumber apprentice, and finished as a project construction engineer. This all thanks to the Soviet power.

This is a wonderful Exhibition! Having walked through it, I [feel] as if [I] walked again through my entire life that I consider to be a happy one.

Thank you very much!

This is a good exhibition.

[It is] as if [I] returned to my childhood. It was not all that bad . . . (Visitors' book, *Gifts to Soviet leaders*; Ssorin-Chaikov 2006b)

As I conceptualized both Soviet gifts and these post-Soviet memories, I found it useful to describe from the point of view of the socialist realism of Soviet art that depicted reality from the point of the view of the progressive future. Soviet-era gifts articulated this future in an idiom of gratitude that appeared after the Revolution of 1917 (see chapter 3 and chapter 5) but culminated in the 1930–50s. These gifts thanked the state, the Party, and Stalin "for our happy childhood" and "happy life." If Soviet documents stressed the role of the Party and its leaders as "leading" and "guiding" the country to communist happiness, they nonetheless stayed clear from describing their role as "bearing gifts." It was these gifts of gratitude, by calling themselves countergifts, that postulated socialism as a gift to which they were responses (Ssorin-Chaikov 2006a). In other words, they articulated a teleological temporality of the imminent future in the language of retrospective temporality of countergifts.

What is interesting about the postsocialist commentary of exhibition visitors is that the commentary followed a similar retrospective logic of gift, albeit in a post-Soviet retrospection. This could be described as a socialist realism of memory in which the future-oriented socialist temporality was given through a temporality of loss or of taking away (Ssorin-Chaikov 2013). If Sosnina and I, as curators, used Bakhtin's concept of chronotope to design the exhibition space as the Soviet-era gifts' "new world" (with *new* as in *time* and *world* as in *space* [Ssorin-Chaikov 2006b]), the post-Soviet public articulated postsocialism as a chronotope that marked its different spaces from museum to everyday life by a temporal point of departure from Soviet socialism (Sosnina and Ssorin-Chaikov 2009).

What I suggest here is, first, extending the idiom of gift giving in narratives of loss to places like Katonga. This draws attention to the temporalities of Soviet help (chapter 2), and to the ways in which the remnants of Soviet projects, like the geodesic tower, were treated as merely givens, that is, as resources out there to be used. Second, this idiom also brings home that the sense of incompleteness, the emergent, the open-endedness that is applicable to the postsocialist period in Katonga, which the anthropology of the contemporary invites us to chronicle as an "accompaniment of time" (Rabinow 2011), needs to be complemented by a chronicle of completeness as a construct regardless if it is the history of the future or the memory of the past. Let me now think through the contrast between my Siberian ethnography and the project on gifts to Soviet leaders in terms of relations between temporalities of research and the temporalities that this research charts.

The time of the notebook (ii)

The temporality of my ethnographic record of the day of April 28, 1994 (described above), is first of all a retrospection based on the diary entry that I wrote on the evening of that day. Second, this fieldwork time took conceptual shape after I completed work in local and regional archives—after I was able to see my main ethnographic informants, such as old Nikolai, acting and speaking at Soviet meetings, and after I found Katonga Evenki being quoted in earlier ethnographic materials, dating back to the 1920s or even early 1900s. It was only over time that the degree and the form of the presence of the ethnographic gaze in Evenki social life became apparent. This, in turn, inspired me to think conceptually about the notes I took during fieldwork as actions that were independent of exactly what I wrote down. But just as Evenki invited me to their forest camp and agreed to have ethnographic conversations with me before I had a chance to properly explain what I was doing there, from the start of my fieldwork I also had an intuitive sense of the state effects of my presence.

Morten Pedersen and Morten Nielsen describe such a hunch as "a transtemporal hinge," that brings together phenomena that are "otherwise distributed across time" but remain invisible unless the modulations of time that "constitute a fieldwork space are given analytical attention" (2013: 129). Pedersen and Nielsen are concerned with the imminence of something significant about to take place but that has not yet happened. On the contrary, my hunch of the state time as equivalent to my field notebook time had to do with the historicization of my presence. When I first came to the Siberian north in 1988–89— then a graduate student at the Institute of Ethnography, Russian Academy of

Science—I was already interested in the contemporary (*sovremennost'*) and state institutions like collective farms. This was not, however, a clearly articulated research agenda but indeed just a hunch that I had difficulties explaining, not only to my informants but also at the Institute. It was only during my fieldwork of the 1990s that I developed this as a project about the legacies of the Russian and Soviet state and state knowledge practices.

If this Siberian ethnography started as a project about the present that took conceptual shape through historicization, the temporality of the gifts to Soviet leaders project operates as the converse. It started as a historical project that eventually developed to be also about the post-Soviet present. Let me consider one of the turning points in this transformation of this gift project, which also illustrates how this visitors' book became the afterimage of the state.

One visitors' book commentator found "the modesty of the gifts [on display] from the material perspective" to be striking, "particularly in contrast with what was stolen from Slizka!" The safe of Vice-Speaker of the Russian Parliament, Liubov' Slizka, had been robbed earlier in 2006. The safe allegedly contained diamonds and other gifts worth about $500,000. "Everything exhibited here [at the exhibition *Gifts to Soviet leaders*] is a reflection of genuine feelings of respect for the leaders. But for what services the contemporary leader Slizka received her gold and diamonds! Shame! She, the scrounger, needs to be not robbed but executed by firing squad!" The commenter noted "the rule" that the Soviet leaders followed when they received gifts, regardless of whether the gifts are modest or precious. They "submitted the received gifts [to the state]—this is an international rule." In contrast, "Slizka, who was robbed of gifts and offerings to an official person on the sum of half-million dollars, was able to hide all this, and still remains in her present post so that she can collect new bribes."

This story appeared in several visitors' comments, and the mood—if not always the tone—of this commentary was widespread throughout the response book. This visitor concluded: "It is shame to live like this in a country where everything is stolen and where people live behind iron [fortified] doors and die at the rate of one million people a year." The exhibition thus has become not merely a site of memory but also of commentary on the present. It is these comments that visitors found "striking" and even "educational"; some of them added, after expressing thanks for the exhibition, that they "particularly liked the visitors' response book." In saying so, the visitors performed an important transformation. They put the visitors' book on a par with the exhibition display. They transformed the response book, and in a way the audience itself, into a peculiar artifact that can be viewed and studied like an exhibited object, into a post-Soviet artifact—that is, as simultaneously artwork and ethnographic notebook.

A response book is a standard exhibition feature. But its genre borders on a "complaint book" (*zhalobnaia kniga*), a ubiquitous institution in both Soviet and post-Soviet public contexts such as shops, restaurants, transport stations, et cetera. Just as in Siberian ethnography, such responses become part of a landscape of correspondence with "the power," which also includes letters to "authorities" from the Party to newspaper and journal editors. My identity in Siberia as an ethnographer visiting "on business of state importance" prompted requests to duly "write down" complains from old Nikolai, Vladimir, and many others. But while in this Siberian project I did not deploy this identity performatively, Sosnina and I did so when we experimented with the visitors' response book. There, we posted a note with our contact details and invited "complaints and suggestions" (*zhaloby i predlozhenia*) in the idiom of a standard Soviet complaint book, but we also invited reflections, comments, criticism, and memories.

This is turn made me think that the project's other materials are also reactions—including the very decision of the Kremlin Museum to hold this exhibition (which was, and still is, exceptional for a museum that normally focuses on the Tsarist period). These were also other actions and reactions to be considered: about ten museums united to form a partnership under the umbrella of the Kremlin Museum as the principle institution; the municipality of Moscow municipality "gave" the exhibition a hall for this project rent-free; and the leading Russian investment consortium, the AFK Systemy, acted as the key exhibition sponsor.

Before the exhibition materialized, it had been a research text (Sosnina and Ssorin-Chaikov 2001). When we wrote the exhibition proposal, we also took into account what the museum or sponsors were expecting in order to put forward a convincing case. This illustrates under-researched "social life" (Appadurai 1986) of the research project as a temporality that is as much a response as a proposal, and something received as much as something given. Then there were complex negotiations with artists whom we commissioned to design the exhibition space and with other museums for object loans; there were also managerial negotiations and clarifications. All these decisions, negotiations, reactions, and counterreactions contained views of Soviet socialism; all turned out to be analogous with the exchange of opinion in the exhibition visitors' book and the media; and all parties involved were working out their own postsocialism through these reactions and decisions.

Further, because our research and exhibition was on gift relations with the state, we could not help but notice that by submitting the exhibition proposal to the Kremlin Museum and by helping its Public Relations Office to contact potential exhibition sponsors, *we were giving gifts and eliciting gifts.* This made us sensitive to how this exhibition mimicked its topic—the gift—and how our research conceptualization of the Soviet-era gifts mimicked this post-Soviet context. This mimesis came across to us very strongly when the administration of the Kremlin Museum decided to gift a copy of the exhibition catalog to President Vladimir Putin for his 55th birthday in 2007. This gift was also a *reaction* to our project, albeit unanticipated by us. But this was just one striking instance in which we found the logic of the gift that we explored meandering out of our research and coming full circle into complex gift relations with the state in which we were involved as both researchers and curators. Artistic and research creativity is *gift* (both in a sense of talent and as a product of creativity); museums create public gifts of their exhibitions and collections; the state often is the most prominent patron (gift giver) for these; yet, most state exhibitions today are made possible also by generous support of private sponsors (see Cummings and Lewandowska 2007; and Maraniello, Risaliti, and Somain 2001 on exhibition experiments on this theme).

Knowledge as chronotope

James Clifford opens his essay, "On ethnographic authority" (1983), with a description of the 1724 frontispiece of Joseph-François Lafitau's *Moeurs des sauvages amériquains*. The ethnographer is depicted as a young woman at the writing table, on which there are artifacts from the New World and from classical Greece and Egypt. The ethnographer

> is accompanied by two cherubs who assist in the task of comparison and by the bearded figure of Time who points toward a tableau representing the ultimate source of the truths issuing from the writer's pen. The image toward which the young woman lifts her gaze is a bank of clouds where Adam, Eve, and the serpent appear. Above them stand the redeemed man and woman of the Apocalypse on either side of a radiant triangle bearing the Hebrew script for Yahweh. (Clifford 1983: 118)

Clifford's goal in this essay is to situate something very different from Lafitau: the Malinowskian ethnographic authority of long-term participant observation, where the emphasis on gaze and observation has displaced participation. He links Lafitau with a Geertzean view of culture as a text. Clifford argues, "different secular versions of Lafitau's crowded scriptorial workshop are emerging" (Clifford 1983: 120), with alternative textual strategies that challenge "a deep Western identification of any text's order with the intention of a single author." This, he adds, "was less strong" at the time of Lafitau (Clifford 1983: 140). In the Russian and Soviet context, the subject of Clifford's critique—the practice of long-term participant observation, where the emphasis on observation has displaced the politics of participation—had marginal institutional presence. Where I was doing research, it was writing rather than observation, textuality rather than gaze, and the author who "transcribes rather than originates" (Clifford 1983: 118) that marked as much the interpretive authority of scholar as it did the state authority of ethnographic notebook, the book of responses and other texts that accompanied the two projects that I discussed in this chapter.

I have argued that these notebooks are not merely texts but also material objects that have agency and temporality in a complex space. I have conceptualized this ethnographic space as a site of exchange rather than discourse or a network of people and things—and, in particular, of exchanges of the time of research and state time. But while ethnography appears here as "secular versions of Lafitau's" young woman assisted by a "figure of Time," it is, however, not so much "the bearded figure of Time" of antiquity but instead modernity as time. The now-old regime of "new times" of Soviet modernity marked the role of ethnographer in Siberia and the relations of hospitality and obligations toward an anthropologist. The new "new times" of post-Soviet modernity was at stake in exchanges in a relational sequence of givers and recipients at—and of—the exhibition of gifts to Soviet leaders. In both cases, modernity as time is not something merely "out there" to be explored, in relation to which researchers are merely academic outsiders. Here, Bakhtin's "chronotope of the depicted world" indeed extends beyond text and enters the worlds of the "author, performer, listener, and reader" of these depictions.

But it does so not through the objectivity of science, in which the Bakhtinian "author" is not a creative writer but a reader of external reality. In such a case, the real world as an object of research description is presumed to exist independently from scholarly activity. As a result of such depiction, there would be, ideally, a match between *the world* and *the depicted world*. In the cases I have considered here, the depicted world enters the worlds of its "author, performer, listener, and reader" in a constructivist perspective on knowledge. But in following this perspective, I do not suggest acknowledging that something is constructed makes it untrue. The aim of the anthropology of science is no more to falsify this form of knowledge than the aim of the anthropology of religion is the falsification of religion (cf. Latour 1993). When Donna Haraway reminds us that *fact* is in its Latin root from *facere*, "to do," "to manufacture," "to make"—the implication of which is that *fact* shares its origin with what seems to be its complete opposite, *fiction* (1989: 4–5)—her point is not to state that fact is in fact fiction, but to ask how facts are themselves manufactured and what is manufactured by facts in science and contexts beyond science. Bruno Latour notes that facts in science are like skyscrapers, nuclear plants, sculptures, or automobiles. He goes on to say, "Even more so than in art, architecture, and engineering," science combines "complete artificiality and complete objectivity moving in parallel" (2005: 89). Thus, he argues for a "symmetrical anthropology" in which research laboratories and their facts could be documented in the same way as buildings, computer chips, and locomotives—as "constructions" that "describe the striking phenomenon of artificiality and reality marching in step" (Latour 2005: 90).

But as "marching" implies, new constructs and new objective facts are markers of time. In cases that I have discussed in this chapter—my own ethnography, Siberian collectives, exhibitions—facts of the past, complaints, nostalgia, and aspirations of the post-Soviet public, and the configurations of the gift in museum sponsorship and the state are symmetrical as simultaneously constructions and depictions of socialism and postsocialism. But there is also an inversion in temporal symmetry of description and construction. The objectivist chronotope of knowledge combines a spatial connotation of the objective "outside" in relation to reality that is being explored with a temporal one: the description is also *after* the world, which comes, so to speak, first. A constructivist chronotope has the reality after itself. Taken in this form, constructivism is not merely Cartesian (Ingold 1992) but creationist. Of course, the very point of the anthropology of knowledge is to resituate the knowing subject "inside" the knowable world, rather than being after or before it. But in this perspective, this chronotope of constructivism appears not as something that explains but as something that itself needs explaining. Taken as architectural constructivism or Soviet constructivism, it is as one of the forms of modernity as time.

CHAPTER 5

Hobbes' gift

We, non-Russian aliens [*inorodsty*], the Tungus, illiterate but feeling deeply, deeply honor the Soviet power. We, the aliens of the Third Clan Soviet Meeting bring our "thank-you" to the Soviet power for the help that was provided to us.
. . .
We all desire that the town is built in the mouth of the Tura river. The land is good here—hunting of squirrels will be good . . .
We all are glad about the town, our life will be easier. Commodities will be cheaper [which is good as] we all have gotten poorer in recent years.
We wish to have a hospital, to cure the sick people.
We need a veterinary, to cure the sick reindeer.
We need school, to teach the natives [*tuzemtsy*] so that they themselves become literate and learned. We will be sending children to school. However many years it takes, let them study. (Gosudarstvennyi Archiv Krasnoyarskogo Kraia [State Archive of Krasnoyarsk Region], fond [deposit] 1845, opis' [description] 1, delo [file] 22, list [page] 3)

This is an excerpt from a meeting resolution of the Ilimpea "Clan Soviet," one of the institutions of indigenous governance that came into being in Siberian north not long after 1917. The meeting took place on February 9, 1926, in Chirinda, a trading post to the north of the area where the Evenki "Lenin" was from, and two years after the Soviet leader Lenin died. This resolution registered an overwhelmingly positive response to the new Soviet governmental campaign to construct a "culture base" (*kul'tbaza*) on the Nizhnaia Tunguska, the "Lower Tungus" river in the northern part of the Yenisei river basin. Here as well as across Siberia, the Soviet government was planning to set up a network of outposts where socialist trade ("cheaper commodities") would signal hope for an "easier life" among the exploited, and where schools, hospitals, veterinary science, and hygiene—all that in the language of that time was called *culture* (hence the "culture base")—would be given to the so-called backward and the nonmodern. This was the beginning of the construction of the *new time*—a state order that identified itself with the epochal novelty. This is an instance of what I have analyzed in this book as the "Soviet gifts of modernity."

Gift theory is a useful lens for conceptualizing such forms of rule (cf. Grant 2009). It draws attention to the paternalistic *giving* that comes hand in hand with *taking* control over territory, population, and resources. In the Siberian indigenous case, the giving of Soviet modernization that started with such culture base projects was continuous on a new scale and with new intensity with the imperial giving of Enlightenment and protection, and with the "pacification" (*zamirenie*) under the Tsar's "exalted hand," which was imposed on indigenous fur hunters together with the fur tribute when Russia conquered this region in the late sixteenth and seventeenth centuries (Ssorin-Chaikov 2000, 2017; Konev 2017; Sirina and Davydov 2017). However, in this chapter I will take this Siberian example not back in time to historicize this kind of giving in the Russian empire but forward to temporalize it within the context of Soviet modernity—that is, to address how this idiom of giving explicitly takes a form of time. Two interlinked issues are addressed below.

Gift time has been an important part of virtually all of the temporalities that I have explored in this book, such as linear time of progress, cyclical time of exchange, and the time that seems beyond time—that is, timelessness. Gift time has been one of the key contexts in which I approached temporal multiplicity through relations of change and exchange in the temporalities that I researched (chapter 2 and chapter 3) and in my own research time (chapter 4). But if above I used gift time to discuss these different modalities of *time*, now—first—is the time to ask what kind of *gift* this is.

If gift theory has been illuminating of the forms of rule that work through this kind of giving, second, what concerns me here is the converse: how might a focus on this rule advance gift theory? How, if at all, does this context modify this theory's key assumptions? The concept of gift that I will propose is not

Maussian, although it has a partial affinity with it (Strathern 1991). The Soviet help with which I started above was conceived at the same time as Marcel Mauss' *The gift*; both were socialist projects. Almost at the same time when Mauss published *The gift*, he gave a critical sociological assessment of Bolshevism (Mauss 1992), but this critique came within a shared conceptual space. This is particularly visible in the concluding sections of *The gift*, where Mauss argues that "the state itself, representing the community," had now recognized that the worker who had "given his life and labor to the collectivity" is in a position in which the societal "debt to him" is "not completely discharged . . . by the payment of a salary." This is both a description of, and an argument for, an emergent "state socialism" (*socialisme d'Etat*), inspired by this principle of debt (Mauss 2016: 180).

For Mauss, this principle of debt is not modern but archaic: "to give to each other without sacrificing themselves to the other" is something that "tomorrow, in our so-called civilized world, classes and nations and individuals . . . will have to learn" from "the clan" and "the tribe" (Mauss 2016: 198). This vision of the future-as-a-return was shared across socialist thought. Karl Marx quoted Lewis Henry Morgan's *Ancient society* (1878: 561–62) when he argued, "'the new system' to which modern society is tending 'will be a revival, in a superior form, of an archaic social type'" (Marx 1984: 107). He penned this when he corresponded with Russian socialist Vera Zasulich, who was concerned with legacies of the "archaic" peasant commune in socialist politics. Marx' point was that, "We should not, then, be too frightened by the word 'archaic'" (Marx 1984: 107). This correspondence was published in Soviet Russia in the 1920s, and became highly relevant for Siberian indigenous policies. The design of clan soviets, for instance, was aimed at achieving scientific communism by rooting it in "primitive communism" (Ssorin-Chaikov 2003: 45–72) of indigenous hunters and herders.

But this was a return that needed to be instigated among Siberian primitive communists by an external agency such as so-called Soviet help—just as peasant socialism of Zasulich needed to be approved by Marx. Communism itself may have been both ancient and modern, but explicit political knowledge about it was a kind of modern truth that was affirmed by this link between knowledge as something that one *has* and something that one *gives*. Whoever was capable of giving this knowledge and this help, and this knowledge *as* help, was the one truly capable of having gained it in the first place. Mauss' gift theory stopped short of situating itself as a modality of giving, although it was clearly a part of contemporary "society [that] wants to rediscover the social cell," seeking out "the sentiments of charity, of 'social service,' of solidarity" (Mauss 2016: 181). Furthermore, Mauss bracketed these remarks as conclusions that are "moral" rather than "sociological." Empirically, modernity was beyond his project. As Jonathan Parry (1986: 458) points out, Mauss demonstrated that the archaic gift is the source of modern *contract*, but he did not address the question of what might from this point of view be the modern *gift*. This gap was subsequently filled by anthropological research into gift giving in various modern contexts, from new reproductive technologies to corporate gifts and corporate social responsibility, philanthropy, humanitarianism, and development (see, for example, Cross 2014; Dolan and Rajak 2016; Konrad 2005; Mosse and Lewis 2005; Bornstein 2009; Ong 2006; Stirrat and Henkel 1997; Fassin 2012). What I add here is socialism as a modality of modern gift. But I am also interested in conceptualizing *modernity* as circulating in *gift form*.

Exploring socialist modernity in this perspective presents an additional and interesting challenge. Just as the modern gift is a gap in Mauss (2016), there is no gift theory in the work of Marx, Engels, or Lenin, who were all concerned with commodity relations and redistribution. In what follows below, I argue, first, that the gift language in the state socialist context is not of Marxist theory but of the "Marxist vernacular" that was improvised by countergifts of gratitude. Second, I submit that there is nonetheless a conceptual link between this vernacular and the Marxist theory. This link is, however, not in the theory of giving, but in the theory of taking—of alienation and requisition, and, above all, of taking power. Third, it is in this theory of taking that I will, in turn, highlight a link with the concept of the gift. But this will be not Mauss' gift but that of Hobbes.

Gift and time

For Mauss, gifts create obligations to reciprocate, and the time of these obligations is the first thing that the giver receives back. Before any actual countergifts, the potential obligation of reciprocity appears as a "guarantee" that they will too (Mauss 2016: 114). The gift that is given imposes this certainly as "a time limit" (Mauss 2016: 114). But if, in the case of Mauss' gift, time is given back before countergifts are made, in the example with which I started this chapter, time is given before anything else is given. Mauss' gift is a form of the future, and so is the Soviet help at the 1926 clan soviet meeting. When this meeting registers the "thank-you for the help provided to us," there is no town, no school, no hospital, no veterinary station to be thankful for. There are no "cheaper commodities."

The future culture base is not yet called Tura—as it will be once it is founded and becomes in the 1930s an administrative center of ethnic autonomy for the "small-numbered nationality" (*malochislennyi narod*), which in 1926 are also not yet officially called Evenki. In the 1920s, documents, including such statements of gratitude, still follow the categories of the Russian Empire. Evenki are still called—and call themselves in such Soviet meetings—"Tungus," which is an older colonial name, and still often more generically as *tuzemtsy* ("natives") and *inorodsty* ("non-Russian aliens"). There exist local Soviet institutions, such as clan soviets, but often only on paper and only at times when Soviet instructors visit this area.

This beginning of the new time is a road that is yet to be taken. It is a nomadic route for a "big trip" (*bol'shoi argish*) to socialism, as the Soviet reformer and writer Mikhail Osharov (1935) subsequently put this; he was both a witness and the instigator of these clan soviet meetings in the mid-1920s. It is a road map with "years that equal to centuries," to use the title of the 1984 book by the Evenki politician and historian Vasilii Nikolaievich Uvachan. Such meetings were foundational events in the Soviet narrative of speeding up history.

This is a narrative of time, but what is the time of this narrative (cf. Ricoeur 1984)? Osharov and Uvachan speak of a leap forward, but long after the event. Both give retrospective accounts, literary and historical accounts, respectively. In contrast, the time of the narrative of gratitude at the 1926 meeting (the "thank-you for the help provided to us") is prospective—it comes before the help is actually provided. Soviet documentation of such meetings often notes that they take place on a "forest glade" (Ssorin-Chaikov 2003: 47), as if empty for construction. This help is not the gift of modernity yet but a *promise* of this gift. What happens on February 9, 1926, does not yet "equal to centuries." It is new time only as a promise of new times. This is, so to speak, a credit that the gift givers take in advance: a *gift credit* or "promissory notes" that empires "mete out," as Ann Stoler (2010: 193) puts this in another context. As such, this gift is, on the one hand, the future in the temporality of credit. It is a promise to pay back in time—that is, to deliver what is promised: schools, hygiene, cheaper commodities, etc. On the other hand, the future is here not merely these promised things, but new time itself. Giving new time will potentially mean that the recipients of this gift cease being backward and nonmodern *tuzemtsy* ("natives") and *inorodsty* ("non-Russian aliens"). But this new time interpolates this temporal distinction quite independently from the things that it promises—furthermore, instantly. Louis Althusser describes how modern ideology transforms the individuals into subjects in a similar way: "by that very precise operation . . . which can be imagined along the lines of the most commonplace everyday police (or other) hailing: 'Hey, you there!'" (Althusser 2001: 118).

In other words, this gift time exists in a double time: it is a form of credit time and a form of new time. But this double time is not a double beat within the same time but a collision of two different temporalities. And it is the second (new time) that makes the first (credit time) a strange one. This advance, this promise, this gift credit of the gift of modernity interpolates *recipients* into debt rather than the *donors*. Nothing is there yet in 1926, but the Soviet meetings duly record gratitude for the gift of modernity that is duly expressed by its nonmodern recipients.

In contrast with Mauss, this gift of modernity imposes reciprocity on the receivers before the gift is actually made. This gift is also about rupture and not continuity, with which Mauss was concerned. Is this gift then Maussian at all? This is a pertinent question, as the comparative literature on modern gifts and on developmental modernity in particular, with which this chapter has a visible affinity, takes Mauss as a conceptual foundation. For instance, political scientist Tomohisa Hattori (2003) has applied Mauss to the gift logic of international developmental aid. He argues that this aid produces a hegemonic developmental hierarchy by drawing on Mauss' thesis that the gift "renders the person who has accepted it inferior" (Mauss 2016: 178). Developmental hierarchy is created at the point when receivers *consent* to receiving assistance and, through this, they to consent their "backward" identity. Central to the power relations at play here is "the mechanism of consent," which Hattori sees in formal financial aid agreements between states or between states and international financial institutions. But as an analytical category, "consent" is linked in his analysis with the Marxist concept of hegemony that accounts for forms of domination that do not rely just on force. Hattori gives a Marxist reading of consent through the Maussian notion of contract.

This reading propels gift theory, which was originally developed to explore "stateless societies," to the territory of political thought concerned with the state and international relations. But within the anthropology of the gift, there is a reverse yet symmetrical move: to read Mauss in the context of political theory. Marshall Sahlins argues that the Maussian gift is analogous to the Hobbesian contract. The archaic gift is a "way of achieving the peace that in civil society is secured by the State" (Sahlins 1972: 169). By way of Sahlins and Hattori, we see, first, what Maussian argument takes from political theory, and, second, what it brings back to it. But while this line of argument works well as a way to situate Mauss, for me it does not work as a way to understand the gifts in question. If anything, it shows exactly how Mauss is *not* applicable to the Soviet gift of modernity. Consent is here only a virtue made of necessity. The town, the school, the hospital, etc., of the Nizhnaia Tunguska culture base, are not gifts that its recipients are at liberty to refuse. In Siberia, as across the former Russian imperial space, expressions of gratitude do take place, but gratitude is not the same thing as consent to accept gifts. I see gratitude as form of a countergift. But in this instance, gratitude is a cover, and even the one that does not quite cover that this gift proceeds not merely before, but also no matter if, it is accepted. This gift is in fact a statement of the indisputability of the mark that the revolutionary state makes on its territory. It begins with an installation of a very real fear of wealth requisition. It comes with a specter of taking as much as it comes with the promise of better life. In 1926, Nizhnaia Tunguska River was outside areas where revolutionary requisitions had already taken place. This specter of taking was the unknown where various possibilities flashed. But what was there as a matter of surety, as solid as it is in Mauss, is that the given time, the new time, will be different. In this sense, too, this (gift) is time.

But if the Soviet gift of modernity is not a Maussian gift, perhaps it is not a gift at all? My argument below is that it is. In contrast with Maussian gift, it is akin not to a Hobbesian *contract* but to a Hobbesian *gift*—a unilateral imposition of sovereignty. In this sense, this gift is not the opposite of war but a means of war. As a war by other means, the gift in question is a form of conquest. It is an apparatus of capture.

Gift as war

> These prestations and counterprestations are entered into somewhat more voluntarily, by way of presents and gifts (*cadeaux*), although ultimately they are strictly compulsory, on pain of private or public war.
>
> . . .
>
> To refuse to give—to neglect to invite, as to refuse to take—is equivalent to declaring war; it is to refuse alliance and communion. (Mauss 2016: 62, 75)

Marshall Sahlins argues that the "war" that Mauss flags in these formulations is Hobbes' "Warre." He submits that Mauss, like Hobbes, debates from an original condition of disorder that makes legitimate an order that is established by the gift: "*Essai sur le don* is a kind of social contract for the primitives" (Sahlins 1972: 169). This original disorder, the Hobbesian war of all against all, is more of a theoretical than a historical temporality in the analytics of something else. Neither Mauss' nor Hobbes' argument is about understanding the "primitive" warfare (cf. Clastres 2010). It is not about the historicity of this original state of nature but about order and peace that comes as its negation. If "Warre" did not exist, it had to be invented, that is, "imagined because all appearance is *designed* to repress it" (Sahlins 1972: 173). One might call this the temporality of social theory that postulates the past as a foundation of the analytics of the present. It is "a hidden substructure that in outward behavior is disguised and transfigured into its opposite," namely, "the consent at the base of organized society" (Sahlins 1972: 169).

In the case of the Hobbesian state, this consent, the social contract, takes the form of the voluntary transfer of rights to sovereign power. In the case of Maussian gift, this consent appears as a system of reciprocal obligations. "The gift is alliance, solidarity, communion—in brief, peace" (Sahlins 1972: 169). Furthermore, gift seems to be a kind of contract that is more equal and genuine. There is no Leviathan, no third party "standing over and above the separate interests of those who contract." There is no submission to it, and the potential terror from it. This gift "is no sacrifice of equality and never of liberty" (Sahlins 1972: 170).

Sahlins' analogy between Mauss and Hobbes serves a critical purpose. It is drawn against Mauss' universalism, manifested in the economic notions of contract and return. Sahlins' case in point is Mauss' interpretation of the Maori *hau*, a spiritual power in things that are passed around as gifts and force the person who receives them to reciprocate. After an exegesis of this concept in Maori ethnography, Sahlins observes a contrast. While the Maori sage who gave the concept of *hau* to an early twentieth-century observer, who then became Mauss' crucial source, tried "to explain a religious concept by an economic principle," Mauss understood this the other way around and "thereupon proceeded to develop the economic principle by the religious concept" (Sahlins 1972: 157). The religious concept here is the one akin to a powerful wind that forces gifts to be passed along, and gift wealth not being accumulated in a single place but continuously dispersed throughout the social body. The implication of this is two very different lines of inquiry. One is the exploration of the meanings of the *hau* and other concepts that are at work in societies that are explored by Mauss' gift theory. Here, Mauss' gift theory turns out to be for Sahlins not necessarily the best way to understand Mauss' own ethnographic material. The other line of inquiry concerns the meaning of contract, economy, and reciprocity that are at work in Mauss' gift theory itself. It is the latter that takes Sahlins from Mauss back to Hobbes in showing that the gift theory has a genealogy in the social contract theory. He argues that however problematic this theory is as a window into non-European cultural categories such as *hau*, it is important as a mirror reflecting the working of Euro-American cultural categories.

But this reading is selective. It assumes a genealogy of the concept of gift in Hobbes' discussion of contract. But Hobbes' categories include that of the gift. It is here that the contrast is illuminating. If, for Sahlins, the Maussian gift "is a kind of social contract for the primitives," for Hobbes himself a gift is emphatically not a contract. The gift enters the discussion of the *Leviathan* when Hobbes defines it as a transfer of rights that are not mutual but unilateral:

> When the transferring of right, is not mutual; but one of the parties transferreth, in hope to gain thereby friendship, or service from another, or from his friends; or in hope to gain the reputation of charity, or magnanimity; or to deliver his mind from the pain of compassion; or in hope of reward in heaven; This is not contract, but GIFT, FREE GIFT, GRACE: which words signify one and the same thing. (Hobbes [1651] 1998: 89)

This definition signals economism too, as it is about the return—whether in terms of friendship, reputation, or even "reward in heaven." But it is ultimately about earthly power, as Hobbes sees "perpetual and restless desire of power after power that ceaseth only in death" ([1651] 1998: 66) as a universal human condition. This desire is dangerous and destructive, and can lead to the state of war of all against all, unless the sovereign power (the state) puts an external limit to it. But getting power as the return is not necessarily contractual ("mutual"). There are two fundamental ways of doing so. Contract as a mutual and voluntary transfer of rights is one. The other is not mutual but a unilateral imposition of will of one party to another:

> The attaining to this soveraigne power is by two ways. One, by natural force; as when a man maketh his children, to submit themselves, and their children to his government, as being able to destroy them if they refuse, or by war subdueth his enemies to his will, giving them their lives on that condition. The other is when men agree amongst themselves, to submit to some Man, or Assembly of men,

voluntarily, on confidence to be protected by him against all others. This latter may be called a politicall commonwealth, or commonwealth by institution; and the former, a commonwealth by acquisition. (Hobbes [1651] 1998: 115)

Note that this contrast between contract and force extends to the family. Family as a form of government is not a Rousseau-esque *natural contract* that naturalizes patriarchy (see Pateman 1988). It is a result of a *natural force* that is akin to war. Tellingly, for Hobbes it is a contract that may be gift if it is a promise that turns out to be empty. If this is "words alone," "if they be of the time to come, and contain a bare promise," it is then "a Free-gift and therefore not obligatory."

Obligation

Hobbesian categories need clarification. First, that fact that the gift is "free" on behalf of the giver does not mean that it is altruistic. The gift is free for Hobbes because it comes out of free will of the giver who is not bound by an obligation to give. Second, the gift generates an "obligation" of gratitude on behalf of the receiver. But this receiver's obligation is not contractual. Here is an important categorical difference between obligation in a sense of Mauss and Sahlins, on the one hand, and Hobbes on the other hand. For Hobbes, contract is a result of free will, the right that "consisteth in liberty to do, or to forbear" (Hobbes [1651] 1998: 86). Gratitude is a result of the free gift, but this is a result of dependency or causality, and thus is itself not free: "Gratitude depends on Antecedent Grace; that is to say, Antecedent Free-gift." It is obligatory as in natural law that is, for Hobbes, obligation but not liberty.

In turn, this natural law (*lex naturalis*) is for Hobbes "a precept, or general rule, found out by Reason," that forbids "man" to do what is "destructive of his life" (Hobbes [1651] 1998: 86). We follow natural law not because we are obligated by a contact to do so but because it is reasonable. It is not followed out of free will with which we enter contract but out of force of necessity that we recognize. What is reasonable is obligatory in this sense. Gratitude is one of such natural laws—and a quite high one on the list of these natural laws that Hobbes gives: number four out of nineteen. In other words, it is second to the first three. The first is the law of seeking peace (the first and "fundamental law of nature"). The second is the law to limit one's rights and desires in the interests of peace. The third is the law of justice that follows the second law of limiting one's rights.

The natural law of justice is there so that whatever covenants are made to have the desired peace—what is actually put in place—are not "mere gifts," that is, "empty words." Then follows, as number four, the natural law of gratitude. It is in this place in relation to what is most fundamental, but also as a matter of analogy. Gratitude depends on antecedent grace as "justice dependeth on antecedent covenant" (Hobbes [1651] 1998: 100). At this point of Hobbes' text, grace, or the free gift (in passages I have quoted above) is already discussed in the section of the second natural law. The free gift, I argue, could be seen as one of means to limit one's rights by creating the state.

In other words, gratitude is not natural as in human nature—just as altruism is not a natural property of grace that precedes it. It is natural in a sense that it is reasonable. Naturally, "a man which receiveth Benefit from another of meer Grace, Endeavour that he which giveth it, have no reasonable cause to repent him of his good will" (Hobbes [1651] 1998: 100). To paraphrase Mauss, a gift is voluntary, but the reciprocity that follows is obligatory. It is an *unreciprocated* gift that is a threat of war. This is insubordination: a war in response to gift as conquest. Grace is originally given in order to gain whatever is good for the giver. It is free and naturally selfish. But if the desired good is not achieved—if the giver is frustrated that that goal is not reached—then the state of war persists:

> For no man giveth, but with intention of good to himselfe; because gift is voluntary; and of all voluntary acts, the object is to every man his own good; of which if men see they shall be frustrated, there will be no beginning of benevolence, or trust; nor consequently of mutuall help; nor of reconciliation of one man to another; and therefore they are to remain still in the condition of war; which is contrary to the first and fundamentall law of nature, which commandeth men to seek peace. The breach of this law, is called *ingratitude*; and hath the same relation to grace, that injustice hath to obligation by covenant. (Hobbes [1651] 1998: 100; emphasis added)

Ingratitude

In chapter 2, I examined a case of the disappearance of a load of combined fodder. The fodder is itself an instance of the help that I describe here as the gift of modernity. I looked at how the linear time of progress as an idiom of this gift was disrupted, first, by cyclical infrastructural difficulties in getting it to

Katonga, and, second, by the particular event in focus: its wasteful expenditure in a series of drinking parties. I discussed how the collective farm director talked to me about Evenki backwardness and also about much more than backwardness, which for him transpired in this event: about things sliding into chaos that is historically stable and incorrigible. This was about not merely sliding back in time, but into another time altogether. I called it a Hobbesian state of nature not in the sense of the war of all against all, but of this state of disorder. In chapter 2, I used this example to illustrate the relations of change between a linear temporality of Soviet developmental time and this Hobbesian timelessness. But now we can put together the full political theory of this event. If help is the Hobbesian gift, it is no wonder that the source of anger of this Leviathan in miniature—the collective director, as we can call him—was his conviction that Evenki, including the Evenki "Lenin," were ungrateful "for the help provided." I argued that the collective order, just as Christian conversion before that, was easy to impose but difficult to maintain. The ingratitude here indicated that the state of war persisted despite initial and rushed expressions of gratitude. But if, as Sahlins put this, the original state of war was a matter of imagination—it had to be invented if it did not exist because "all appearance is *designed* to repress it" (Sahlins 1972: 173)—the war that was after and not before this order—the fundamental ingratitude, the waste of development, and the waste of developmental time—was a real struggle, even if consisting not in fighting but in this chaos. I argue elsewhere that from the time of the imposition of the fur tribute on the seventeenth century, pacification was an endemic problem after the conquest, in subsequent governance, rather than the problem to be solved by the initial conquest (Ssorin-Chaikov 2000, 2003). If help is a Hobbesian gift that is a form of conquest, ingratitude is a way to resume the war.

War as time that extends beyond wartime

Sahlins is right that there is a mirroring of Hobbes and Mauss. Gratitude or countergifts appear "somewhat voluntary" but are in fact "strictly compulsory, on pain of private or public war" (Mauss 2016: 62). It is at this point that Mauss introduces time as the imposed limit for reciprocation that happens at the threat of another potentiality: war. This is the time that is also war for Hobbes. But for Hobbes, war is not merely an imagined original state: for him, peace as a way to defer the potentiality of war is still war. War is a form of time that extends beyond the actual wartime:

For WAR consisteth not in battle only, or the act of fighting; but in a tract of time, wherein the will to contend by battle is sufficiently known: and therefore the notion of *time*, is to be considered in the nature of war; as it is in the nature of weather. For as the nature of foul weather, lyeth not in a shower or two of rain; but in an inclination thereto of many dayes together; So the nature of war, consisteth not in actual fighting; but in the known disposition thereto, during all the time there is no assurance to the contrary. All other time is PEACE. (Hobbes [1651] 1998: 84; emphasis in original)

Thus, peace is not when war is only potentiality a threat. War as potentiality is war nonetheless. Peace is all other times that are not "actual fighting" and also not "disposition thereto." It is the notion of peace, not war, that frames this discussion: the first and "fundamental law of nature" is the law of seeking peace. It is an end in time, and not the beginning in time, and also another, alterative temporality that runs through conquests, wars, contracts, gifts, and countergifts. This other time, which is peace, is an alternative time, a futurity, to which Hobbes' observation that "during all [this] time there is no assurance to the contrary" is also applicable in a symmetrical way as it is to the time of war. This disposition is an "assurance," as Hobbes puts this; or, in the words of Mauss, it is the "surety" of relatedness that comes in the form of countergifts, as what Hobbes calls gratitude. Thus, whatever these countergifts are as things, they are also time:

"Time" is necessary to fulfill every counterprestation. The notion of a time limit is therefore logically implied when it comes to paying visits, contracting marriages and alliances, brokering peace, attending games and organized combat, celebrating rotating festivals, rendering ritual services of honor, "displaying reciprocal respect," all the things that one exchanges, at the same time as other more and more numerous and precious things, as these societies grow more wealthy. (Mauss 2016: 115)

Gift gives this time limit that is the time of peace. After countergifts are made, parties can call it quits, alliances end, and war is resumed. But before—and instead of—this imaged finality, "societies become wealthier," as in these feasts of reciprocity the time limits (futures) are exchanged "at the same time as other more and more numerous and precious things" (Mauss 2016: 115).

Mauss (2016: 122) posits a triple unity of obligations: to give, to receive, and to reciprocate. But Mauss does not discuss the first or original gift. To give already appears as an obligation. It is unclear how this is so if the bond that is presumably established by gift giving does not exist yet. Although his view is widely understood as illuminating how sociality is created, it is not a perspective on how this creation actually happens—how the social appears in the first instance, out of something else. Mauss posits total services or presentations as already existing before gifts. "We do not deal with in this text," he plainly states, with giving and sharing in "its most ancient form, that of total prestation" (Mauss 2016: 115). On the contrary, Hobbes is concerned with the first, foundational "free gift": the gift that does not follow any "antecedent grace." His free gift is the first act in particular relations, if not necessarily the first ever, original gift.

Gift perspectivism

Yet Hobbesian gratitude may well generate not only its own gifts but also a narrative of the first gift to which it is a response. For instance, gratitude may include a statement that the first gift is in fact a genuine charity, and not at all conquest. It also may put forward an alternative view of human nature—that, for instance, that it is altruistic, or that the total services are already in place. This could be in contradiction to a Hobbesian view that humans are naturally selfish but at the same time perfectly "reasonable" within the Hobbesian logic of gratitude that should not repent the giver of his good will. In other words, the pair of free gift and gratitude form singularities, each with their own logic that is folded into themselves yet equally total. Let's call this "perspectivism" (Viveiros de Castro 1998) within gift relations. This perspectivism is simultaneously temporal and narrative (Ricoeur 1984). Gratitude is a narrative of an event and an event of narrative. In this exchange of free gift and gratitude there is also an exchange of their temporalities, a case in point in exchange relations within temporal multiplicity, which I discuss in this book. The first temporality unfolds from the first free gift to gratitude, with the latter being antecedent in the sense of Hobbes. This is a temporality of natural force, the "state by acquisition"; this is war as actuality or potentially. The other temporality is gratitude. The latter retrospectively constructs the gift to which it is a response, its meanings, and the intentions of the giver. What is given back is a whole narrative of gift relations that unfold from the original gift. But this is the gratitude's narrative. Let me illustrate this with an example.

Vernacular Marxism

Ural mountains. Siberian forests. In the beginning, wild Siberia was inhabited by stone warriors. This [being made of stone] is clearly easier for such a warrior: he would not be beaten by animals, or caught by heat or cold.

The riches of Siberia were under a warrior's mitten, in a topaz glass under the guard of Cashfullov[1] the warrior [*bogatyr' Denezhkin*] and his helper, the stone magpie.

Warriors grew old. Moss began to grow on them and they themselves began to turn into mountains. Cashfullov also got senile, but he kept his watchful eye on the glass [with the riches of Siberia].

[Much time passed.] Plowmen and hunters started to appear in Siberia.

Soon those came, who started digging the ground looking for something that was put there for usefulness. Having heard about Cashfullov's topaz glass, they asked him to lend them some money.

"Take as much as you need," rattled Cashfullov like thunder in distant mountains, "but on condition that it is spent on the good of the people." But the diggers would drop their picks and spades, and grab [the riches] with envy and force.

No longer they would ask the warrior to take off his mitten, [instead] they struggle and sweat to move it a little, get the gold, and run away. They would die but would not leave the [stolen] riches.

After that, the stone magpie helper would collect the [abandoned] sacks of gold, pour the gold back to the glass and drop the [empty] sacks nearby.

There were some lucky getters [who managed to get away with the gold]. But when was the time for them to think of the good of the people if they were busy filling their pockets and currying favors with the Czar? Such were the pretty-pretties on which the Ural riches were spent!

Then a man appeared walking across taiga. This was a simple-looking man although dressed in an urban fashion. He approached the warrior, and asked if there isn't anything there put for the good of the people. The warrior sparkled: "You are the one I am waiting for!"

Cashfullov explained to him the meaning of the stone coins, and rattled, as if he was young, like thunder in distant mountains: "Listen you, the one who understands the final words of the old stone mountains: take the glass in response. You have cheered me up." And [as he said this] he became a mountain.

---

1.   I thank Catriona Kelly for suggesting this translation of *Denezhkin*.

"I will do," said the man, "and if I won't be in time [to fulfill the promise] over the course of my life, I will pass this task to use the riches for the good of the people to a trusted man." He lifted the warrior's mitten as if it was light, and covered the glass. And he became himself huge, and left.

And the farther away he went, the more visible he became so that neither mountains nor forests can overshadow his figure from sight.

And then the people's country started to be built. Combines went out into the collective farm fields. Soviet science came all the way to the very depth of the Ural mountains. And the country is led along the Lenin's path by a trusted man, J. V. Stalin. (Karluchenko 2006)

This text, entitled the "Warrior's mitten," originates in a collection of Urals fairy tales, *The malachite casket*, part-collected, part-composed by socialist activist and folklorist Pavel Bazhov (1879–1950). This particular version was shortened as a plot for a china set made at the Baranovo porcelain factory, Ukraine. Each paragraph of this text was inscribed on the bottom of each of the set's pieces to explain the scene that was depicted on this piece (see figs. 6a–i). Lenin is the person who approached the warrior. In the text, he does not have to be named; he is depicted on the china. But he is also unnamed in the original printed version (Bazhov 1944).

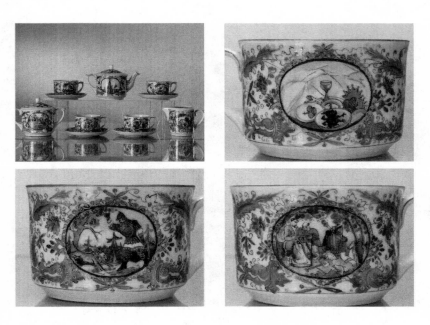

Figure 6a–i. China set with the motifs of P. P. Bazhov's tale, "Warrior's mitten." Gift to I. V. Stalin for his 70th birthday from the collective of the Baranovo Porcelain Factory, 1949. *Courtesy of the Central Museum of Contemporary History of Russia.*

This china set was presented as a gift to Stalin in 1949, on the occasion of his seventieth birthday, from the Baranovo porcelain factory workers. This is a vivid example of the narrative construction of the original gift of socialism by the gift of gratitude. This gift is just one example of a mass flow of gifts on that occasion, from all corners of Soviet society and communist movements from around the world (Ssorin-Chaikov 2006a). This particular china set marks the time of Stalin's anniversary, which itself marks the time of socialist modernity, with the gift time of Urals mythology. Bazhov modifies this story's supposed folklore origins with the figure of Lenin as culture hero. Lenin, by taking the gift of the riches, completes the making of both a nature and a culture. Nature is finally made when the stone warrior turns into a mere mountain after he passes the treasure to Lenin. The culture is made when the so-called usefulness of this wealth is realized in the country that is being built, collective farm combines working the fields, and scientists exploring the mountains. The porcelain version of this story, in turn, modifies Bazhov by adding the last line—that Stalin, the "trusted man," is leading the country along Lenin's path.

But the porcelain version also adds a visual image that also very considerably modifies the story, and in fact takes it from the folklorized idiom of official Soviet culture to what I call "vernacular Marxism." In the original published text, the wealth that was guarded and passed from hand to hand is the primordial riches of the Urals. They are called "money," "stone money," and "small coins made of various local precious stones and ore." They have power to make things transparent, and signify potentiality. It was the money that gave the warrior his name, Cashfullov (*Denezhkin*). What is drawn on china is somewhat different. There are coins in the glass on some of the scenes, but the images of the treasure (the source of Lenin's gift of socialism) include things that are hardly so primordial and magical. On one of the cups we see a pile consisting of the Tsar's crown, imperial two-headed eagle, icons, crosses (see fig. 6b). This is wealth of the old regime, the revolutionary loot.

This loot is an addition to the natural riches of Siberia, and the two together make the picture of these gifts strikingly similar to the scene that American businessman Armand Hammer depicted when he wrote his first account of his Russian trips of the 1920s, entitled *The quest of the Romanoff treasure* (Hammer 1932). These are the Urals' precious stones and metals that lie idle, as was the asbestos mine that Hammer saw and ended up using in his first Soviet concession, which I described in chapter 3. Additionally, there are art and antiques from the Hermitage and other Russian art collections, most of them former Tsar's family property. Hammer was quick to get involved in the trade of this art in the West, which the Soviet government in the 1920s was eager to use in the same fashion as the Urals' valuables: as a resource that is simply there, free for use.

The "Romanoff's treasure" is the wealth on which the narrative of Hammer's gifts and the narrative of the "Warrior's mitten" china set converge (fig. 7). Lenin turns *this* into the gift of socialism. As in Mauss' *hau*, the spirit of this gift cannot stay idle. There is already a *giftness* in these riches. They could be used "for the good of the people" by Lenin because they were put there "for usefulness." The question is exactly what this giftness or usefulness is. If inside

Figure 7a. Book cover of Armand Hammer's *The quest of the Romanoff treasure.*
New York: W. F. Payson, 1932.

Figure 7b. A cup from china set with the motifs of P. P. Bazhov's tale, "Warrior's
mitten." Gift to I. V. Stalin for his 70th birthday from the collective of the Baranovo
Porcelain Factory, 1949. *Courtesy of the Central Museum of Contemporary History of Russia.*

the "Warrior's mitten" are the natural riches of Siberia, without the "Romanoff's treasure," this is nature's gift. It is already there as a gift by virtue of merely being *given*. If, however, the inside of the "Warrior's mitten" is the "Romanoff's treasure," it is then a gift by virtue of being *taken*. In the outset of this chapter, I described the Tungus "gratitude for the help provided to use" in which taking (requisitions) was still a potentiality. The china set actually alludes to this taking. This allusion speaks volumes in the Soviet context, given its requisitions, terror, and other forms of Hobbesian conquest. Taking makes the Hobbesian giftness of this treasure. But this allusion is also to the Marxist understanding of this taking. The gift is a *return* to the people who are, from this point of view, the treasures' original owners. The loot is a retaking of what was taken away.

This is a straightforward Marxist perspective. Wealth is a product of labor, not nature before human labor: it is the creation of the working people. By virtue of this labor, it is rightfully theirs. At this point, Karl Marx' labor theory of value is Lockean. The difference with John Locke becomes apparent in Marx' discussion of what happens after this right of ownership is socially recognized. For Locke, this recognition is a basis of contractual relations between owners of property. It is the same matter of "liberty" as in Hobbes. Property includes products of labor but also labor itself; contractual relations include those of sale of such properties. But Marx argues that this perspective overlooks that the actual contract conditions are never equal and free. The sale of labor has historically been a buyers' market—that is, a market in which it is the buyers who determine the market value of labor. Throughout *Capital*, and in particular in chapters on primitive accumulation and colonialism, Marx shows that capital introduces slavery where "free" labor market cannot be assured, for example, by laborers who have no other property in possession than their labor and thus have no other option but "freely" selling it for a wage. One of his examples is of a certain Mr. Peel, who exported to Australia his factory and the workers but who upon arrival was immediately left with no workers as they abandoned him to become farmers on abundantly available land.

"Unhappy Mr. Peel," exclaims Marx sarcastically, "who provided for everything except the export of English modes of production to Swan River" (Marx 1996: 544). But Marx' fundamental argument is that wherever this labor market is free, it is so only euphemistically. Labor market is a buyers' marker. The sale of labor is not Hobbesian "liberty" but Hobbesian "obligation" that follows the force of natural law. This force is visible not in the same overt and brutal form as in slavery. This is force of what is "reasonable": workers *understand* that they have no other choice. The free labor market is established through a threat of hunger (Polanyi 1944); and the material regeneration of workers' energy and physical conditions is what for Marx underpins the logic of his labor theory of value. But I argue that if Marx' labor theory of value has a Lockean view of property, this force of free labor market is a Hobbesian conquest. "What is the crime of robbing a bank in comparison with the crime of founding a bank," asks Bertolt Brecht's character in the *Threepenny opera* (1928). This revolutionary taking, the requisition, is Lenin's gift of seizure, before it is put to proper use for the good of the people.

But in understandings of this state of war, of requisition and seizure, Marxist theory and Marxist vernacular are not Hobbesian because the original state is not war but peace. The chain of exchanges that ends with the gift of socialism starts with alienation of labor from workers as its true owners. But once upon a time, this labor was not alienated. The products of work and relations of productions were not estranged from the worker and worker's collectivity. Just as in Hobbes and Mauss, this original condition is speculative as it is posited by the understanding of the subsequent history of alienation and inequality. But, to paraphrase Hobbes, this peace is in a tract of time wherein the will to contend by peace is sufficiently known.

Vernacular Marxism as a gift theory

Unlike Hobbes, Marx and Lenin do not elaborate on the gift. The closest we get to it is Lenin's remarks on help and assistance that the Party and the working class ought to provide to "the backward peoples" so that they bypass capitalism en route to the communist future (see chapter 2). Mauss remarks that "state socialism" recognizes that moral obligations to the worker "are not completely discharged by the payment of a salary." For him, social insurance is a mark that "our ethics and our lives" still exist within the morality of gift (Mauss 2016: 178). But Mauss' argument is not Marxist; it's syndicalist. Jean Baudrillard attempts, in the 1970s, to merge Maussian and Marxist perspectives in a view of capital giving the gift of labor to the worker before taking it back for a wage (Baudrillard 1993). Both Mauss and Baudrillard outline the space of modern gift politics. For Mauss, capitalism remains obligated to the workers even after the wages are paid; for Baudrillard, the workers cannot return this original gift of labor and therefore cannot cancel the power of the capitalist, unless they do a semiotics of exploitation (Baudrillard 1993: 36–43). But for Marx and Lenin, capitalist hierarchies are givens, rather than gifts. They are givens as matters of knowledge that require praxis, including violent practice. But this notion that knowledge is a gift, and that the new world that follows this knowledge is a gift, is articulated not by Marxist theory but by a Marxist vernacular of gratitude. The sources of this gift theory are not Marx or Lenin, or even Stalin but the "masses" that are encompassed and constructed by the Soviet project of Hobbesian conquest. This idiom of gratitude originates under Lenin (Tumarkin 1987) but is magnified as dominant in countergifts to Soviet leaders for the gift of socialism. An important trigger here is Stalin's 1935 remarks, that "life has become better, more joyous." While, as Stalin stressed, this happened under the guidance of the Party, neither Stalin nor other Soviet leaders have described this "leading role" as gift giving. What calls socialism a gift is the countergift of gratitude, thanking the leaders, and Stalin in particular, "for our happy life" (Ssorin-Chaikov 2006a; see also Brooks 2001).

The gift of socialism is this Marxist vernacular, as is the gift of knowledge. Lenin of the "Warrior's mitten," walking through the forest "dressed in an urban fashion," is an iconic scholarly figure who has the gift of knowledge together with gifts as the Party organizer and workers' leader. But in the "Warrior's mitten," this knowledge is a gift of nature, "the final words of the old stone mountains," that is passed to Lenin. Bazhov's own longer textual version of this story stresses that the riches are actually knowledge. They are surely "money" but more importantly they are signs that have the power "to show the place" where there is much more of it:

> The glass is obviously of the warrior's size. It is higher than human height, and much higher than a forty-bucket barrel. It is made of the best golden topaz and honed utmost thinly and clearly. The ore and precious stone money [that is in the glass] is seen through [it], and the power of this money is such that it shows the place. If the warrior takes the money, rubs it from one side, momentarily the place where the money's ore or stone is from appears in sight—it is there for spotting and knowing with all its hills, valleys, and swamps. The warrior would take a look at it, in order to inspect if all is well there, and then rub another side of the money to illuminate another place. There, it would become as clear as a

drop where the ore is, and how much of it is there. The other ores and stones would be obscure. In order to see them, one needs to take [and rub] other money from the same place. (Bazhov 1944: 670)

When Lenin in this fuller version of this story inspects the inside of the warrior's mitten, he is amazed "how cleverly this is thought through," and adds: "If this is figured out properly, all this land could be made known in advance [*napered*]—just come and sort it according to the order [*razbirai po poriadku*]." Russian *razbirat'* is simultaneously "to sort" and "to take," and *razbirai po poriadku* has a double meaning of "sorting it according to the order" and "taking it one by one."

This is more than knowledge: it is transformative truth. Once Lenin takes it away, "the people's country started to be built." Combines go out into the fields and Soviet science comes to the Urals. This knowledge is light—as in this power to see, to make mountains transparent. This idiom was widely rehearsed by other gifts, quite literally as Enlightenment as a vision, such as the 1923 gift to the 13th Communist Party Congress from the workers of an electric lamp factory who manufactured a light bulb with a filament in the form of Lenin's figure with raised hand pointing forward (see fig. 2, p. 6). Furthermore, this Marxist vernacular casts meaning on gifts that were manufactured elsewhere and in different times but ended up in this Soviet space. Recall Hammer's gift to Lenin of a sculpture that was made circa 1893: the ape sitting on the works of Darwin, holding compasses with the toes of one of its feet, and contemplating a skull that it holds with a hand (see fig. 1, p. xvi). The sculpture's Latin inscription reads "You will be as gods" (*Eritis sicut deus*), which acquires a Marxist meaning by virtue of being a gift to Lenin and a part of the display of the Museum of the Lenin's Flat and Study in the Kremlin (see chapter 3).

But it was this gift, when displayed in 2006 as a part of the exhibition of gifts to Soviet leaders, that triggered Hobbesian interpretations from this exhibition's audience. In chapter 4, I discussed some of this audience's responses in the book of comments. In contrast with those, the sculpture *Eritis sicut deus* was one of gifts that some of the visitors thought to be offensive. During interviews with the visitors that I conducted together with Olga Sosnina during of this exhibition, they commented that "we are not apes" and that "while Lenin thought of us as apes, he is himself now in the zoo." By this, a Moscow teacher in her 50s referred to numerous images of Lenin in the glass boxes of this exhibition. But *zoo* evokes the Soviet gift of modernity as an apparatus of capture. Historian Robert Payne conveys such a vision of the Soviet experiment in conclusion of his famous biography of Lenin. For Lenin, "All men are apes; they must move about at his [Lenin's] bidding, or else they become skills. They must me trained and herded into schools, to receive the instructions of the schoolmaster. They must not dispute with him or with any of his ancestors, for freedom to dispute is not granted to them. He demands mindless obedience because, being apes they are mindless and deserve no better fate" (Payne 1964: 62930).

It is telling that Payne expresses this view when discussing the meaning of the same sculpture, *Eritis sicut deus*: "On Lenin's desk in the Kremlin there stood, for most of the years he worked there, a strange bronze statue of an ape gazing with an expression of profound bewilderment and dismay at an oversize human skull" (Payne 1964: 626). Why, he wonders, was this "dubious ornament" that would appeal only to "a bourgeois taste," with "its very ugliness and vulgarity contributing to its popularity" among "middle classes," there in the same Lenin's study as were the portraits of Karl Marx and Stepan Khalturun? (Khalturun was an icon of radicalism in Russia after he organized a bomb explosion in the Winter Palace in an attempt to assassinate Tsar Alexander II, escaped the police, and was arrested and executed only subsequently, when he assassinated the Odessa public prosecutor). Why, Payne asks, the placement of this sculpture in Lenin's study—exactly where "a deeply religious man would have placed a crucifix, a state of Buddha, or some other symbol that represented his faith?" (Payne 1964: 628).

Payne's take on the meaning of this gift is consistent with his reading of Lenin's character, which he sees as rooted in the ruthlessness of revolutionary underground, pragmatism of exile, and the violence of the Revolution and Civil War. But this meaning is in the shadow not just of Lenin's personality but also of Soviet history and Soviet society, with subsequent purges, the gulag, and the collectivization. "Lenin had many sins," he continues, "but the gravest was his supreme contempt for the human race" for it is "in the nature of science to be inhuman." Lenin was perfectly prepared to regard "men . . . as statistics, or as trends or as obstacles standing in the path of his scientific dictatorship" (Payne 1964: 630, 628).

The notion of "scientific dictatorship" is interesting. It suggests not merely Hobbesian "perpetual and restless desire of power that ceaseth only in death," which so often assumed in totalitarian approach to Soviet modernity, but also an ardently zealous modernism of truth. What Lenin so often called the "iron logic" of history, the revolutionary legality and constructivist legitimacy of building the new world, is a Hobbesian violent sovereignty of natural law. Lenin's gift of modernity is that of the reasonable and thus absolutely necessary, a domain where there is no liberty, not because it is not *liberal* but because it is an *obligation* in the sense of Hobbes.

CHAPTER 6

Modernity as time

This book's subtitle, *A brief anthropology of time*, refers to the book's length, but also to one of its key aspects—to the time of anthropology, and in particular the time of reading anthropology. The act of abbreviation, putting things "in short," contributes to the relations between different temporal registers that bridge the temporalities that anthropology studies and the temporalities of anthropology itself. This book is an artifact of these temporalities. One has to be "brief" and fast, not merely in terms of the tempo of change in a reality that is being described (where, however, ethnographic writing is more likely to lag behind [Marcus 2003]) but also in terms of confronting the challenges of academic communication in which writing is far more condensed in comparison with Malinowski-era monographs. Briefness here is a form of exchange between the temporalities we explore, the temporalities of ethnography, and the temporalities of argument.

Throughout this book, I stressed that my goal in discussing these temporalities is primarily methodological. But already in the previous chapter I moved to some substantive conclusions. I argued that the gift time of the Soviet "gifts of modernity" reveals a particular logic of gift relations that are Hobbesian rather than Maussian. This raises a broader question: what are configurations of modernity (Western and Soviet) that are visible in relations between temporalities and among various agents and institutions that I explored here?

This question is important, as temporality has been one of the crucial tools for understanding modernity as a distinct condition, associated with mass industrial production, bureaucratic procedures, forms of the state and its ideologies, techniques of the self, et cetera. This book enters quite a crowded analytical space where Karl Marx' classic observation that capitalist modernity annihilates space by time (Marx 2008: 539–40), rubs shoulders with E. P. Thompson's (1967) analysis of the importance of time for the formation of modern discipline and subjectivity, Anthony Giddens' (1984) theory of structuration, David Harvey's (1989) discussion of "just in time" global production, etc.—as well as specific discussions of temporalities of socialist modernity (e.g., Verdery 1996; Hanson 1997; Buck-Morss 2000; Gumerova n.d.). How is this book situated in this rich and diverse body of scholarship?

In brief, what I add is the suggestion to approach modernity not merely as a distinct condition that *has* a particular temporal order but, rather, as itself a form of time. Charles-Pierre Baudelaire ([1863] 2010: 33), who is credited with coining the very term *modernity*, defined it as a state of being that is constantly transient, fleeting, and contingent. But to be in such a state of modernity is also to be "of modern time," to exist on history's cutting edge. This vanguard is simultaneously a condition of possibility of modern systems of production, bureaucracy, and discipline and, at the same time, one of its products—a commodity, an identity, and the self. In this context, to think of modernity as merely a state or condition that *has* a distinctly modern temporality would be somewhat tautological. This would amount to stating that an order of time has an order of time. But this also would be essentializing modernity as something existing as if separately from the forms of time that it "has." On the contrary, modernity as time (which is the formulation that I suggest) seems to be a case par excellence of Nancy Munn's (1983: 280) acute observation that sociocultural systems do not simply go on *in* or *through* time but *are* themselves time.

My argument in this concluding chapter will be about some of the implications of the notion of modernity as time, which include, first, that this temporality is a multiplicity, and second, that it is a device that temporalizes social typologies. This argument has affinity with Reinhart Koselleck's (2002) conceptual history of modernity. One of his examples lies in the German-language context, where *modernity* is literally *newtime* (*Neuzeit*) and where it appears approximately at the same time as Baudelaire's *modernité*. It is not merely a "new time" (*neue Zeit*) when things are changing, or a condition that acknowledges that change has taken place. Newtime is a kind of time that is characterized by "an open future": "The emphatic use of the expression 'new time' was not only sustained by previous inventions, innovations, and discoveries that, on looking back, would have conferred an entirely new shape to the world, but this concept was likewise directed at the future in which new things would continue to come about" (Koselleck 2002: 165).

It has been long established that modernity produces a particular view of time as "uniform, infinitely divisible, and continuous" (Sorokin and Merton 1937: 616). But modernity as a *newtime* isn't itself just a position in this kind of time, but also time's distinct quality. It is the present, marked by a constantly "open future," that is, as a moment of constant epochal distinction of *now* and *before*. Sebastian Conrad, in this account of the making of global time as an extension of the modern clock time, notes a contradiction between the epochal time of modernity, which is about rupture, and the everyday modernist temporalities, which are about continuities (Conrad 2016). In chapter 1, I gave the example of the Soviet calendar reform of 1918 that adopted the Gregorian calendar, thereby eliminating a two-week time difference with the Julian calendar that Russia had previously followed. It is this homogenization that introduced a gap between chronological and socialist epochal time. The "Day of the Great October Socialist Revolution" that happened on October 23, 1917, was now to be celebrated in November. In chapter 5, where I discussed modernity as time taking form of the Hobbesian gift, I started with a brief example of the construction of the early Soviet "culture base" on in Central Siberia. This base's school, hospital, etc., has eventually brought about the homogeneous and objectified clock time as well as distinctly socialist new calendars, temporalities of compulsory work, or equally compulsory waiting time of queuing and state rituals that Katherine Verdery (1996: 39–58) conceptualizes as the "etatization of time." But Hobbesian giving is a foundational rupture that both temporarily precedes all these varieties of modernist temporalities and also, more importantly, exists in a different temporal register. This highlights that what modernity *is* as time differs from the time that modernity *gives* and *takes*. It follows that if modernity produces homogeneous and objectified chronological time, this very temporal perspective is insufficient for understanding modernity itself. As a temporalization device, modernity is not just something homogeneous that takes over a local temporal multiplicity but is itself constitutive of multiplicity.

Temporalization

Koselleck points out that while the term *modernity* is coined in in the second half of the nineteenth century, its key notion of the present as an "open future" retrospectively captures changes that were taking place since the eighteenth century. He agues that in this process one can see a particular temporality, such as a belatedness of conceptual development in relation to what these concepts describe, but also a "temporalization of history." Modernity as *newtime* becomes foundational for the retrospective elaboration of not just itself but also epochal differences, such as those of the Middle Ages, the Renaissance, and the Reformation—as well as the epochal, and not just chronological, concept of "century." Koselleck finds it "striking" how new ways of designating such temporal differences have "gained acceptance and been consolidated in shorter and shorter spans of time." He notes that it took some time to coin and elaborate the concept of the Middle Ages as extending over seven hundred to eight hundred years. However,

> in comparison, the Reformation and the Renaissance were not only much more quickly accepted as periodizing concepts, but they also indicated correspondingly shorter temporal units. The concept of capitalism, following upon and corresponding to the concept of feudalism, was only coined in the second half of the nineteenth century so that the new experiences that had amassed since the Industrial Revolution could be much more quickly conceptualized than the comparatively contourless, long-lasting stretch of so-called feudalism. Here, *a similar rhythm of the shortening of time* can be found again in the determination of periods, as we have observed with the employment of the other concepts in the span from the sixteenth through the eighteenth centuries. (Koselleck 2002: 164; emphasis added).

It is this classificatory impulse that seems to me clearly linked with the briefness that I mentioned above. But the temporalities of contemporary field ethnography as well as the tempo of anthropological writing are related today to something that Koselleck does not consider: an increasing speed in which the new ages of today, rather than the ages of history, are identified in social theory. Classificatory categories of "late capitalism," "postmodernity," "globalization," "the contemporary," etc., are all attempts to specify historical novelty against the background of what by now appears not as modernity's "an open future" but, conversely, as its retrospective predictability a slower time of "the Enlightenment project" (which is not just longer but also "comparatively contourless," to use Koselleck's words, as it may include everything form Foucault's "classical age" to Soviet socialism) and also, more recently, of deep time and anthropocene.

In other words, the argument about modernity as time that I develop in this book is not just a way to approach socialist modernity but also to reread, from a new angle, current anthropology's temporalization of the contemporary. This book's outline of the workings of the Soviet *newtime* is an intervention at a time when anthropology is itself increasingly focused on the new. This interest has been expanding in the second half of the twentieth century, but one of its very clear turning points was a "spatial turn" of the late 1990s that critically addressed previously "assumed isomorphism of space, place and culture" (Gupta and Ferguson 1997a: 34). What is interesting for me is that this concern with space has also been a concern with time. It situated itself "at the end of an era" (Gupta and Ferguson 1997b). It was a form of reflection on the (un)bounding social space of transition from *modernization* to *globalization*. A notion of multisited ethnography was, for example, a way to understand the new shape of the world that was constituted "in a piecemeal way, integral to and embedded in discontinuous, multi-sited objects of study" (Marcus 1995: 97). Laying open *previously* taken-for-granted assumptions about isomorphism of place, culture, and "the field" not only drew attention to but, it is argued, was enabled by cultural forms that are *today* "nonisomorphic with standard units of analysis" (Collier and Ong 2005: 3). A "shift from two-dimensional Euclidean space, with its centers and peripheries and sharp boundaries, to a multidimensional global space with unbounded, often discontinuous and interpenetrating sub-spaces" (Kearney 1995: 548) is a shift in time.

But investigations into these taken-for-granted assumptions about space leave unquestioned assumptions about time that enable this methodological reformulation. Anna Tsing (2000) remarked that this perspective conceptually restates a cultural narrative that globalization tells about itself: that of the radical epochal break between *before* and *now*. But there is more than that. However unique this particular shift may be, it is also understood within a frame of a culturally neutral linear time that frames conceptualization of this new space. Linear time is posited as an objective measure of difference and a means of classification and discursive distribution of the global, whether we agree that modernity is no longer organized in "tightly territorialized, spatially bounded, historically self-conscious, or culturally homogenous" units (Appadurai 1991: 191; Hannerz 1989); or if we support a contrary view that the ecumenes of "interconnected space . . . always already existed" (Gupta and Ferguson 1997a: 37; Friedman 1994); or if we maintain "different historical moments" of global processes "cannot be linked in a developmental or teleological sequence" (Maurer 2000: 690–61).

If this culturally neutral linear time appears here as a measuring device, what is a time frame that enables more recent formulations when time has been explicitly added to space? What are temporal assumptions of a kind of anthropology that turned toward the study of the "here and now," rather than "far-away" and "timeless" (Rees 2008: 7)? I leave aside an important question of exactly where, and whose is this *here* and focus on the *now*. Its new properties emerge when "anthropologists experience profound temporal turbulences"—when (and because) they "can *no longer* make assumptions about what is necessary for their method to produce rich ethnographic data—a temporally stable scene and subject of study" (Rees 2008: 7; emphasis added). The contemporary is marked by a time when "no single sensibility—modernist or otherwise—dominates, overarches, or underlies current affairs" (Rabinow 2008: 78; see also Rabinow 2011). It is impossible, on the one hand, "to inquire into what is taking place" by "deducing it beforehand" (Rabinow 2008: 3). On the other hand, its cultural orientation on the present is marked by what Jane Guyer (2007) described as an "evacuation of the near future"—such as stable career prospects and the reliability of either market economy or social welfare—in contrast to the infinitely deferred far-away and almost timeless horizon of the neoliberal market finally balanced or religious salvation taking place. In other words, the present time is marked by a nonlinear and unstable *presentism*.

To put this briefly, this turn to the here and now marks a double departure. Here, a departure of anthropology from non-Western or "traditional" societies to modernity coincides with a departure of modernity itself from a "Euclidian" stable time (Kearney 1995). As I elaborated in chapter 4, this double transformation is easily described as a shift or a "time's arrow" (Hodges 2008) or "straight time" (Boellstorff 2007). George Marcus and Paul Rabinow suggested two contrasting ways of designing the anthropology of the contemporary, respectfully, around the notions of connection and flight. One historicizes it by looking at genealogies of the present—for instance, the present of anthropology coming "home," driven by all kinds of historical reasons—while the other stresses an unprecedented novelty of the present as an object of research and its irreducibility to these historical links with the past. But what I suggest here is looking at the temporal frame—or indeed at the multiplicity of temporal frames—that underscores this very distinction. This, in turn, illuminates a different kind of genealogy in this perspective. This is not merely a genealogy that might link, for example, the contemporary of the early twenty-first century with the early twentieth-century socialist notions of new time that I discuss in this book, or with a Baudelaire-esque sense of modernity as being constantly transient, fleeting, and contingent, or with Koselleck's "open future," which goes back to the eighteenth century. Rather, what becomes apparent is that in their very interest in new, emergent forms, these anthropological debates retain a familiar (albeit much criticized in other contexts) temporal analytic of time and the other.

This is despite, or perhaps indeed because, this discursive orientation is no longer backwardness (Fabian 1983) but novelty: "*new* forms of cultural difference and *new* forms of imagining community" (Gupta and Ferguson 1997b: 36; emphasis added). The exploration of this new world could be performatively Malinowskian (Boellstorff 2008). However, overall it is not quite performatively realist and historicist—and in this regard this move is not in continuity but in a sharp contrast with the reflexive turn of the 1980s that has engendered these subsequent shifts. It is within this frame that what I would call *new time as the other* assumes ethnography to be a linear chronicle of constant changes and turbulences (Rabinow 2008, 2011). It is this chronicle that is always late (Marcus 2003). As Hirokazu Miyazaki and Annelise Riles note, it is its conceptual incompleteness in which "a retreat from knowing" affirms "that little can be known about the world except for the fact of complexity, indeterminacy, and openendedness" (2005: 327). In other words, it is this chronicle's failures that ultimately affirm this new world's otherness. This incomprehensibility looks historically symmetrical with the constitution of the so-called primitive in early anthropology (Hodgen 1965). But if in early anthropology this incomprehensibility was a starting point, here it is an endpoint.

However, let me reiterate that the point of approaching these debates through the lens of modernity as time is not just to historicize this new time as the other. If anything, it is to highlight that this historicization itself needs to be approached through the lens of the anthropology of time. The difference in question is between temporalizing—that is, highlighting exact differences in time and degrees of novelty—and exploring the work of temporalization. If modernity as a condition that *has* a particular temporal organization is a product of such temporalization, modernity as time is a temporalizing device. Looking at the former allows us to compare and contrast modernity with societal orders that are *not* modern, as well as distinguish *early-*, *high-*, *late-*, and *post-* modern forms, or modernity's distinct types, such as capitalist and socialist (cf. Kotkin 2001; Fitzpatrick 2005; David-Fox 2015). Exploring the latter illuminates how temporalization becomes a mode of relatedness. In the cases that I discussed throughout this book, modernity as time illuminates the making of Soviet-style hierarchies that are both internal and external. In Siberia, they distinguish the *modern* from the *backward* and the *traditional* (cf. chapters 2, 4, and 5). I dem- onstrated that whether or not the Evenki "Lenin" is a "contemporary Evenki" matters for how relatedness around him is structured. But for Lenin (the Soviet leader), modernity as time is a contested claim at the global stage. At stake in this kind of temporalization is what and who is truly modern, who is truly "ahead." These claim's categories are not *modern* versus *premodern* but *modern* versus *modern*. Soviet socialism, for instance, tried to position itself as an alter- native modernity vis-à-vis capitalism. "To reach and overtake [America]" was to become one of the most popular industrial slogans of the 1930s. There were good arguments both of the Soviet and the post-Soviet era that Soviet socialism in fact lagged behind capitalism in many crucial aspects, such as work efficiency, quality of goods, and the quality of life, and that there were only some select areas such as math, space exploration, ballet, et cetera where it could be said it was leading. But neither this nor the acknowledgment of nuclear parity really changes the point of view from which the argument is made: modernity as a *true* difference in time, and in this Soviet versus Western instance (unlike in the case of technological and other differences between Western or Soviet-style economies and societies), this difference is epochal. What was debatable here was *who* was ahead; what was shared was this time perspective. The temporiza- tion in this case takes the shape of a sequence or movement from one form of alternative and true modernity to another—what I call here the relations of change, which include the perestroika of the 1980s and post-Soviet transitions of the 1990s and the early 2000s.

The state, commodity, and gift

The implication of this approach to understanding socialist modernity is not just that it is a case of the "etatization of time" (Verdery 1996: 39–58). It is also the converse: what one might call a "temporalization of the state." Katherine Verdery charts how time was used by state socialism as a state-building resource in a fundamentally political process. It takes the explicit and coercive form of the "seizure of time" (Verdery 1996: 40) while also working more subtly through the everyday politics of time. But I have shown that this "seizure" was also con- strued as giving. There is a symmetry of the seizure of time and of the Soviet "given time" (Derrida 1992)—and indeed, not just symmetry but exchange be- tween these temporalities (see chapter 3) and of giving and taking (chapter 5). I argue that the politics of time in question include those of the Hobbesian gift—that is, of the gift as a form of conquest and entrapment. I demonstrate that these politics of time also include wasteful expenditure—as in the episode of the waste of the combined fodder—and the politics of identity of this temporality of waste as Hobbesian timelessness, an incorrigible state of nature (chapter 2).

In 1980s Romania, what constituted Verdery's (1996) case in point as to the etatization of time was that time was needed as a resource in order to re-pay Western loans and survive in the self-imposed regime of austerity. In this regard, Verdery's discussion and the reality that she focuses on, can be seen as being ahead of its time, as it is precisely the time of debt and austerity that becomes a very widespread form of temporalization (cf. Engelen et al. 2011; Guyer 2012; Dyson 2014; Blyth 2013). "Financialization" has become a global currency; it is political as much as it is economic, a new form of entrapment by modernity as time.

But what I explore articulates not merely a link between state time and commodity time. This link can be good to think about alterity of capitalism versus socialism or their analogy: the time of Romanian loans and the contemporary financialized debt, or novelty as a commodity or the state. But one of the temporalities in question is not just the time of commodity and the time of centralized state redistribution (Polanyi 1944; Verdery 1991) but also the *time of the gift*. We understand quite well how the *giving* of modernity happens in commodity form—how modernity is sold, bought into, and consumed. But this giving also takes the form of a gift of new time—as we saw in the aesthetics of the *Eritis sicut deus* sculpture (chapter 1), the Leninist notions of help (chapter 2), and the Hobbesian gift (chapter 5).

Of course, this gift is not exclusively Soviet. As in the aesthetics of the sculpture *Eritis sicut deus*, with which I opened this book (see fig. 1, p. xvi), gifts of empire (Grant 2009) include both Christian and Darwinian "civilizing missions." They temporalize imperial order as an assemblage of different stages of development. What I call the Soviet *gift of modernity* partially repeats this imperial ordering, which is visible, for instance, in the temporalization of the identity of Evenki "Lenin" from his own statements that he is "contemporary Evenki" to the collective farm's director conviction that he is a like "a wolf who looks back the forest no matter how long it is fed." But at the time of Lenin-the-Soviet-leader, this partial repetition of imperial ordering happens in a pe-culiar form of anti-empire. In space (in relationship to Western powers) and in time (in relation to prerevolutionary Russia), Lenin battles out anti-imperialism militarily and theoretically. *Imperialism* for Lenin equals *capitalism* at its high-est, last stage (he thinks)—despite his reliance on foreign specialists, including Armand Hammer, and despite his fascination with Fordism. Marxist-Leninism is a theory of the modern commodity—and only afterward a theory of modern empire. A Marxist theory of colonization—either in the respective chapters of Marx' *Capital* or Lenin's *Imperialism*—is a theory of the commodity extended to the theory of colonial socioeconomic and political forms. Marxism is famously laconic on exactly what communism is. But socialism and communism as "new-time" temporalizes in great detail capitalism and imperialism as the "other in time." This temporalization is, in turn, an instant "flashing," in a sense of Doreen Massey (1992: 80) of another "other time." My final, brief example of modernity as time and the gift will be a 1923 gift, which I used for this book's cover. The workers of the United First and Second Electric Lamp Factory presented the 12th Congress of the Russian Communist Party (of Bolsheviks) with a material artifact of a Leninist vision. This is a gift of an electric light bulb with a fila-ment in the shape of Lenin (see fig. 2, p. 6). It gives a striking image of "Lenin's light," which at that time symbolized bringing a predominantly peasant Russia out of the darkness of villages with no electricity. Lenin's hand points forward, setting the direction of Enlightenment. But socialism is itself here a gift of light, a marker of new time.

References

Abu-Shams, Leila, and Araceli González-Vázquez. 2014. "Juxtaposing time: An anthropology of multiple temporalities in Morocco." *Revue des mondes musulmans et de la Méditerranée* 136: 33–48.

Adam, Barbara. 1998. *Timescapes of modernity: The environment and invisible hazards*. London: Routledge.

Alexievich, Svetlana. 2013. *Vremya sekond khend*. Moscow: Vremia.

Althusser, Louis. 2001. "Ideology and ideological state apparatus." In *Lenin and philosophy, and other essays by Louis Althusser*, 85–126. New York: Monthly Review Press.

Anderson, Benedict. 1983. *Imagined communities*. London: Verso Books.

Anderson, Mark M. 1992. *Kafka's clothes: Ornament and aestheticism in the Habsburg fin de siècle*. Oxford: Oxford University Press.

Appadurai, Arjun, ed. 1986. *The social life of things: Commodities in cultural perspectives*. Cambridge: Cambridge University Press.

———. 1991. "Global ethnoscapes: Notes and queries for a transnational anthropology." In *Recapturing anthropology: Working in the present*, edited by Richard G. Fox, 191–210. Santa Fe, NM: The School of American Research.

———. 1996. *Modernity at large: Cultural dimensions of globalization*. Minneapolis: University of Minnesota Press.

Armitage, David. 2015. "Horizons of history." *History Australia*. 12 (1): 207–25.

Badiou, Alain. 2005. *Being and event*. London: Continuum.

Bakhtin, Mikhail. 1975. *Voprosy literatury i estetiki: Issledovaniia raznykh let*. Moscow: Khudozhestvennaia literatura.

Barbusse, Henri. 1920. *La lueur dans l'abime: Ce que veut le groupe Clarté*. Paris: Clarte.

————. 1935. *Stalin: A new world seen through one man*. London: John Lane

Baudelaire, Charles-Pierre. (1863) 2010. *The painter of modern life*. London: Penguin Books Limited.

Baudrillard, Jean. 1993. *Symbolic exchange and death*. London: Sage.

Bazhov, P. P. 1944. "Bogatyreva rukavitsa." *Novyi Mir* 8&9: 67–69.

Bear, Laura. 2014. "Doubt, conflict, mediation: The anthropology of modern time." *Journal of the Royal Anthropological Institute* 20 (S1): 3–30.

Beer, Gillian. 2000. *Darwin's plots: Evolutionary narrative in Darwin, George Eliot, and nineteenth-century fiction*. Cambridge: Cambridge University Press.

Bergson, Henri. 1965. *Duration and simultaneity: With reference to Einstein's theory*. Indianapolis, IN: Bobbs-Merrill.

Bestor, Ted. 2001. "Supply-side sushi: Commodity, market, and the global city." *American Anthropologist* 103 (1): 76–95.

Birth, Kevin K. 2012. *Objects of time: How things shape temporality*. New York: Palgrave Macmillan.

Blumay, Carl, and Henry Edwards. 1992. *The dark side of power: The real Armand Hammer*. New York: Pocket Books.

Blyth, Mark. 2013. *Austerity: The history of a dangerous idea*. Oxford: Oxford University Press.

Boas, Franz .1974. "The principles of ethnological classification." In *A Franz Boas reader*, edited by George W. Stocking, 61–67. Chicago: University of Chicago Press.

Boellstorff, Tom. 2007. *A coincidence of desires: Anthropology, queer studies, Indonesia*. Durham, NC: Duke University Press.

————. 2008. *Coming of age in second life: An anthropologist explores the virtually human*. Princeton, NJ: Princeton University Press.

Bogoras, Waldemar. 1925. "Ideas of space and time in the conception of primitive religion." *American Anthropologist* 27 (2): 205–66.

Bogoraz (Tan), V. G. 1923. *Einstein i religiia: primenenie printsypa otnositel'nosti k issledovaniiu religioznykh iavlenii*. Petrograd: Izdatel'stvo L.D. Frenkel'.

Bornstein, Erica. 2009. "The impulse of philanthropy." *Cultural Anthropology* 24 (4): 622–51.

Bourdieu, Pierre. 1991. *The logic of practice*. Stanford, CA: Stanford University Press.

Brandisauskas, Donatas. 2016. *Leaving footprints in the Taiga: Luck, spirits, and ambivalence among the Siberian Orochen reindeer herders and hunters.* Oxford: Berghahn.

Briggs, Jean L. 1970. *Never in anger: Portrait of an Eskimo family.* Cambridge, MA: Harvard University Press.

Brooks, Jeffrey. 2001. *Thank you, Comrade Stalin! Soviet public culture from revolution to Cold War.* Princeton, NJ: Princeton University Press.

Bruk, Mikhail. 1964. "He talked to Lenin." *Soviet Life* 103 (4): 9.

Buck-Morss, Susan. 2000. *Dreamworld and catastrophe: The passing of mass utopia in East and West.* Cambridge, MA: MIT Press.

Burbank, Jane. 1995. "Lenin and the law in revolutionary Russia." *Slavic Review* 54 (1): 23–44.

Callon, Michel. 1986. "Some elements of a sociology of translation: Domestication of the scallops and the fishermen of St. Brieuc Bay." In *Power, action, and belief: A new sociology of knowledge?*, edited by John Law, 196–223. London: Routledge.

Canales, Jimena. 2015. *The physicist and the philosopher: Einstein, Bergson, and the debate that changed our understanding of time.* Princeton, NJ: Princeton University Press.

Chakrabarty, Dipesh. 2000. *Provincializing Europe: Postcolonial thought and historical difference.* Princeton, NJ: Princeton University Press.

Chelcea, Liviu. 2014. "Post-socialist acceleration: Fantasy time in a multinational bank." *Time & Society* 24 (3): 1–19.

Clastres, Pierre. 2010. *Archeology of violence.* New York: Semiotext(e).

Clifford, James. 1983. "On ethnographic authority." *Representations* 2:118–46.

Collier, Stephen J., and Aihiwa Ong. 2005. "Global assemblages, anthropological problems." In *Global assemblages: Technology, politics and ethics as anthropological problems*, edited by Aihiwa Ong and Stephen J. Collier, 3–21. Oxford: Blackwell.

Conrad, Sebastian. 2016. *What is global history?* Princeton, NJ: Princeton University Press.

Cooper, Frederick, and Randall M. Packard, ed. 1997. *International development and the social sciences: Essays on the history and politics of knowledge.* Berkeley: University of California Press.

Cross, Jamie. 2014. "The coming of the corporate gift." *Theory, Culture & Society* 31 (2–3): 121–45.

Cummings, Neil, and Marysia Lewandowska. 2007. "From capital to enthusiasm: An exhibitionary practice." In *Exhibition experiments*, edited by Sharon Macdonald and Paul Basu, 132–53. Malden, MA: Blackwell.

Dalsgaard, Steffen, and Morten Nielsen. 2013. "Introduction: Time and the field." *Social Analysis* 57 (1): 1–19.

David-Fox, Michael. 2015. *Crossing borders: Modernity, ideology, and culture in Russia and the Soviet Union*. Pittsburgh, PA: University of Pittsburgh Press.

Deleuze, Gilles. 2004. *Difference and repetition*. London: Continuum.

Derrida, Jacques. 1992. *Given time: 1. Counterfeit money*. Chicago: University of Chicago Press.

Dick, Hilary Parsons. 2010. "Imagined lives and modernist chronotopes in Mexican nonmigrant discourse." *American Ethnologist* 37 (2): 275–90.

Dickerman, Leah. 2001. "Lenin in the age of mechanical production." In *Disturbing remains: Memory, history, and crisis in the twentieth century*, edited by Michael S. Roth and Charles G. Salas, 77–110. Los Angeles: Getty Research Institute.

Dolan, Catherine, and Dinah Rajak, eds. 2016. *The anthropology of corporate social responsibility*. Oxford: Berghahn Books.

Draper, Theodore. 2003. *The roots of American communism*. New Brunswick, NJ: Transaction.

Durkheim, Emile. 1960. *Montesquieu and Rousseau: Forerunners of sociology*. Ann Arbor: University of Michigan Press.

Dyson, Kenneth. 2014. *States, debt, and power: "Saints" and "sinners" in European history and integration*. Oxford: Oxford University Press.

Engelen, Ewald, Ismail Ertürk, Julie Froud, Sukhdev Johal, Adam Leaver, Mick Moran, Adriana Nilsson, and Karel Williams. 2011. *After the great complacence: Financial crisis and the politics of reform*. Oxford: Oxford University Press.

Engels, Friedrich. 1989. "Karl Marx' funeral." In *Collected works*, by Karl Marx and Friedrich Engels, vol. 24, 467–72. Moscow: Progress Publishers.

———. 1991. "Engels to Pyotr Lavrov [12-17 November, 1875]." In *Collected works*, by Karl Marx and Friedrich Engels, vol. 45, 106–110. Moscow: Progress Publishers.

Epstein, Edward Jay. 1996. *Dossier: The secret history of Armand Hammer*. New York: Random House.

Escobar, Arturo. 1995. *Encountering development: The making and unmaking of the third world*. Princeton, NJ: Princeton University Press.

Evans-Pritchard, E. E. 1940. *The Nuer: A description of the modes of livelihood and political institutions of a Nilotic people*. Oxford: Clarendon Press.

Fabian, Johannes. 1983. *Time and the other: How anthropology makes its object*. New York: Columbia University Press.

Fassin, Didier. 2012. *Humanitarian reason: A moral history of the present*. Berkeley: University of California Press.

Ferguson, James. 1994. *The anti-politics machine: "Development," depolitization and bureaucratic power in Lesoto*. Minneapolis: University of Minnesota Press.

Fitzpatrick, Sheila. 2005. *Tear off the masks!: Identity and imposture in twentieth-century Russia*. Princeton, NJ: Princeton University Press.

Fournier, Marcel. 2006. *Marcel Mauss: A biography*. Princeton, NJ: Princeton University Press.

Franklin, Sarah. 2014. "Rethinking reproductive politics in time, and time in UK reproductive politics: 1978–2008." *Journal of the Royal Anthropological Institute* 20 (S1): 109–25.

Friedman, Jonathan. 1994. *Cultural identity and global process*. London: Sage.

Geertz, Clifford. 1966. *Person, time, and conduct in Bali: An essay in cultural analysis*. New Haven, CT: Yale University Press.

———. 1973. *The interpretation of cultures*. New York: Basic Books.

Gell, Alfred. 1992. *The anthropology of time: Cultural construction of temporal images and maps*. Oxford: Berg.

Giddens, Anthony. 1984. *The constitution of society: Outline of the theory of structuration*. Cambridge: Polity Press.

Gillette, Philip S. 1981. "Armand Hammer, Lenin, and the first American concession in Soviet Russia." *Slavic Review* 40 (3): 355–65.

Graeber, David. 2001. *Toward an anthropological theory of value: The false coin of our own dreams*. New York: Palgrave.

———. 2011. *Debt: The first 5,000 years*. New York: Melville House.

Grant, Bruce. 1995. *In the Soviet house of culture: A century of perestroikas*. Princeton, NJ: Princeton University Press.

———. 2009. *The captive and the gift: Cultural histories of sovereignty in Russia and the Caucasus*. Ithaca, NY: Cornell University Press.

Greenhouse, Carol J. 1996. *A moment's notice: Time politics across cultures*. Ithaca NY: Cornell University Press.

Groys, Boris. 2003. *Iskusstvo Utopii. Gesamtkunstwerk Stalin. Stat'I*. Moscow: KhZh Pragmatika Kul'tury.

Gumerova, Mariia. n.d. "Predposylki, rezul'taty I effekti reform sotsial'nogo vremeni v SSSR (1920–nachalo 1930kh godov)." (Dissertation manuscript)

Gupta, Akhil, and James Ferguson, eds. 1997a. *Anthropological locations: Boundaries and grounds of a field science*. Berkeley: University of California Press.

———. 1997b. "Culture, power, place: Ethnography at the end of an era." In *Culture, power, place: Explorations in critical anthropology*, edited by Akhil Gupta and James Ferguson, 1–32. Durham, NC: Duke University Press.

Guyer, Jane I. 2007. "Prophecy and the near future: Thoughts on macroeconomic, evangelical, and punctuated time." *American Ethnologist* 34 (3): 409–21.

———. 2012. "Obligation, binding, debt and responsibility: Provocations about temporality from two new sources." *Social Anthropology* 20 (4): 491–501.

Hammer, Armand. 1932. *The quest of the Romanoff treasure*. New York: W. F. Payson.

Hammer, Armand, and Neil Lyndon. 1987. *Hammer*. New York: Putnam. Hannerz, Ulf. 1989. "Notes on the Global Ecumene." *Public Culture* 1 (2): 66–75.

Hanson, Stephen E. 1997. *Time and revolution: Marxism and the design of Soviet institutions*. Chapel Hill: University of North Carolina Press.

Haraway, Donna. 1989. *Primate visions: Gender, race, and nature in the world of modern science*. London: Routledge.

Harvey, David. 1989. *The condition of post-modernity: The enquiry into the origins of cultural change*. Oxford: Basil Blackwell.

———. 2005. *A brief history of neoliberalism*. Oxford: Oxford University Press.

Hattori, Tomohisa. 2003. "Giving as a mechanism of consent: International aid organizations and the ethical hegemony of capitalism." *International Relations* 17 (2): 153–73.

Hobbes, Thomas. (1651) 1998. *Leviathan*. Oxford: Oxford University Press.

Hobsbawm, Eric. 1995. *Age of extremes: The short twentieth century, 1914–1991*. London: Viking Penguin.

Hodgen, Margaret T. 1965. *Early anthropology in the sixteenth and seventeenth centuries*. Philadelphia: University of Pennsylvania Press.

Hodges, Matt. 2008. "Rethinking time's arrow: Bergson, Deleuze, and the anthropology of time." *Anthropological Theory* 8 (4): 399–429.

Ingold, Tim. 1992. "Culture and the perception of the environment." In *Bush base, forest farm: Culture, environment, and development*, edited by Elisabeth Croll and David Parkin, 39–56. London: Routledge.

Karluchenko, N. 2006. "Serviz po Motivam Skaza P.P. Bazhova 'Bogatyreva Rukovitsa': Podarok I.V.Stalinu K Ego 70-Letiu Ot Kollektiva Baranovskogo

Farforovogo Zavoda Im. V.I.lenina, 1949 G." In *Dary Vozhdiam/Gifts to Soviet leaders*, edited by Nikolai Ssorin-Chaikov, 182. Moscow: Pinakotheke. Exhibition catalogue.

Kasatkin, Ivan. 1919. *Lesnaia Byl'. Rasskazy*. Moscow: Izdatel'stvo VTsIK.

Kearney, Michael. 1995. "The local and the global: The anthropology of globalization and transnationalism." *Annual Review of Anthropology* 24:547–65.

Kharitonova, E. N. 1980. *Ot Vsego Serdza: Podarki V.I. Leninu*. Moscow: Izobrazitel'noe Iskusstvo.

Konev, A. Iu. 2017. "Dar, dan' i torgovlia: antropologiia vzaimideistvia avtokhtonov Sibiri i russkikh v XVII–XIX vv." *Etnograficheskoe Obozrenie* 1:43–56.

Konrad, Monica. 2005. *Nameless relations: Anonymity, Melanesia, and reproductive gift exchange between British ova donors and recipients*. Oxford: Berghahn.

Koselleck, Reinhart. 2002. *The practice of conceptual history: Timing history, spacing concepts*. Stanford, CA: Stanford University Press.

Kotkin, Stephen. 2001. "Modern times: The Soviet Union and the interwar conjuncture." *Kritika: Explorations in Russian and Eurasian History* 2 (1): 111–64.

Kunetskaia, L., and K. A. Mashtakova. 1979. *Lenin: Great and human (Based on materials and exhibits displayed in Lenin's Kremlin study and flat)*. Moscow: Progress Publishers.

Latour, Bruno. 1993. *We have never been modern*. Cambridge, MA: Harvard University Press.

———. 2005. *Reassembling the social: An introduction to actor-network-theory*. Oxford: Oxford University Press.

Latour, Bruno, and Steve Woolgar. 1986. *Laboratory life: The construction of scientific facts*. Princeton, NJ: Princeton University Press.

Lavrillier, Alexandra. 2005. "Nomadisme et adaptations sédentaires chez les Evenks de Sibérie postsoviétique: 'Jouer' pour vivre avec et sans chamanes." PhD diss., Ecole pratique des hautes etudes.

Lazar, Sian. 2014. "Historical narrative, mundane political time, and revolutionary moments: Coexisting temporalities in the lived experience of social movements." *Journal of the Royal Anthropological Institute* 20 (S1): 91–108.

Leach, Edmund. 1961. *Rethinking anthropology*. London: Athlone Press.

Lefebvre, Henri. 2004. *Rhythmanalysis: Space, time, and everyday life*. New York: Continuum.

Lenin, Vladimir Ilyich. 1970a. "Beseda s delegastiei Mongol'skoi narodnoi respubliki 5 noiabria 1921 goda." *Polnoe sobranie sotchinenii*, vol. 44, 232–33. Moscow: Izdatel'stvo Politicheskoi Literatury.

———. 1970b. "Luchshe men'she, da luchshe." *Polnoe sobranie sotchinenii*, vol. 45, 389–406. Moscow: Izdatel'stvo Politicheskoi Literatury.

———. 1970c. "O vnutrennei i vneshnei politike respubliki. Otchet VTsIK i SNK 23 dekabria 1921 goda" *Polnoe sobranie sotchinenii*, vol. 44, 291–329. Moscow: Izdatel'stvo Politicheskoi Literatury.

———. 1970d. "Zakliuchitel'noe slovo po dokladu o prodovol'stvennom naloge, 27 maia 1921 goda." *Polnoe sobranie sotchinenii*, vol. 43, 317–32 Moscow: Izdatel'stvo Politicheskoi Literatury.

———. 1971. "Razvitie kapitalizma v Rossii." *Polnoe sobranie sotchinenii*, vol. 3. Moscow: Izdatel'stvo Politicheskoi Literatury.

———. 1981. "Doklad komissii po natsional'nomu i kolonial'nomu voprosam II kongressa Kommunisticheskogo internatsionala." *Polnoe sobranie sotchinenii*, vol. 41, 241–48. Moscow: Izdatel'stvo Politicheskoi Literatury.

Lévi-Strauss, Claude. 1987. *Introduction to the work of Marcel Mauss*. London: Routledge and Kegan Paul.

Maraniello, Gianfranco, Sergio Risaliti, and Antonio Somain, eds. 2001. *Il dono: Offerta, ospitalità, insidia*. Milan: Charta.

Marcus, George E. 1995. "Ethnography in/of the world system: The emergence of multi-sited ethnography." *Annual Review of Anthropology* 24:95–117.

———. 2003. "The unbearable slowness of being an anthropologist now: Notes on a contemporary anxiety in the making of ethnography." *XCP: Cross-Cultural Poetics* 12 (12): 7–20.

Marcus, George E., and Fred R. Myers, eds. 1995. *The traffic in culture: Refiguring art and anthropology*. Berkeley: University of California Press.

Martens, L. K. 1958. "Vospominania o V. I. Lenine." *Istoricheskii arkhiv* 1 (5): 146–50.

Marx, Karl. 1984. "Drafts of a reply to Vera Zasulich (February/March 1881)." In *Late Marx and the Russian Road: Marx and "peripheries of capitalism,"* edited by Teodor Shanin, 99–122. New York: Monthly Review Press.

———. 1996. "Capital, Volume I." In *Collected works*, by Karl Marx and Friedrich Engels, vol. 35. Moscow: Progress Publishers.

———. 2008. *Grundrisse: Foundations of the critique of political economy*. Philadelphia: Taylor & Francis.

Massey, Doreen. 1992. "Politics and space/time." *New Left Review* 196: 65–84.

Maurer, Bill. 2000. "A fish story: Rethinking globalization on Virgin Gorda, British Virgin Islands." *American Ethnologist* 27 (3): 670–701.

Mauss, Marcel. 1992. "A sociological assessment of Bolshevism." In *The radical sociology of Durkheim and Mauss*, edited by Mike Gane, 165–212. London: Routledge.

———. 2016. *The gift: Expanded edition*. Chicago: HAU Books and University of Chicago Press.

May, Jon, and Nigel Thrift, eds. 2003. *Timespace: Geographies of temporality*. London: Routledge.

McTaggart, J. M. E. 1908. "The unreality of time." *Mind* 17 (68): 457–84.

Mellor, D. H.1998. *Real time II*. London: Routledge.

Mitchell, Timothy. 1998. "Fixing the economy." *Cultural Studies* 12 (1): 82–101.

Miyazaki, Hirokazu. 2003. "The temporalities of the market." *American Anthropologist* 105 (2): 255–65.

Miyazaki, Hirokazu, and Annelise Riles. 2005. "Failure as an endpoint." In *Global assemblages: Technology, politics, and ethics as anthropological problems*, edited by Aihiwa Ong and Stephen J. Collier, 320–31. Oxford: Blackwell.

Morgan, Lewis Henry. 1878. *Ancient society; or, Researches in the lines of human progress from savagery, through barbarism to civilization*. New York: H. Holt.

Mosse, David, and David J. Lewis. 2005. *The aid effect: Giving and governing in international development*. London: Pluto.

Munn, Nancy. 1983. "Gawan Kula: Spatiotemporal control and the symbolism of influence." In *The Kula: New perspectives on Massim exchange*, edited by Jerry W. Leach and Edmund Leach, 277–308. Cambridge: Cambridge University Press.

———. 1992. "The cultural anthropology of time: A critical essay." *Annual Review of Anthropology* 21: 93-123.

Nil, Archiepiskop Iaroslavskii. 1874. *Putevye Zapiski*. Iaroslavl': Tipografia Gubernskoi zemskoi upravy.

Noll, Richard, and R. A. Segal. 1994. *The Jung cult: Origins of a charismatic movement*. Princeton, NJ: Princeton University Press.

Odom, Anne, and Wendy R. Salmond. 2009. "Introduction: From preservation to the export of Russia's cultural patrimony." In *Treasures into tractors: The selling of Russia's cultural heritage, 1918–1938*, edited by Anne Odom and Wendy R. Salmond, 3–34. Seattle: Hillwood Estate, Museum & Gardens; distributed by University of Washington Press.

Ogle, Vanessa. 2015. *The global transformation of time: 1870–1950*. Cambridge, MA: Harvard University Press.

Ong, Aihiwa. 2006. "Corporate players, new cosmopolitans, and Guanxi in Shanghai." In *Frontiers of capital: Ethnographic reflections on the new economy*, edited by Melissa S. Fisher and Craig Downey, 163–90. Durham, NC: Duke University Press.

Ong, Aihiwa, and Stephen J. Collier, eds. 2005. *Global assemblages: Technology, politics, and ethics as anthropological problems*. Oxford: Blackwell.

Osharov, Mikhail. 1935. *Bol'shoi argish*. Moscow: Khudozhestvennaia Literatura.

Parry, Johnathan. 1986. "The gift, the Indian gift and the 'Indian gift.'" *Man* 21 (3): 453–73.

Pateman, Carole. 1988. *The sexual contract*. Cambridge: Polity Press.

Payne, Robert. 1964. *The life and death of Lenin*. New York: Simon and Schuster.

Pedersen, Morten Axel, and Morten Nielsen. 2013. "Trans-temporal hinges: Reflections on an ethnographic study of Chinese infrastructural projects in Mozambique and Mongolia." *Social Analysis* 57 (1): 122–42.

Polanyi, Karl. 1944. *The great transformation*. New York: Rinehart.

Prior, A. N. 1957. *Time and modality*. Oxford: Oxford University Press.

Propp, Vladimir. 1968. *Morphology of the folktale*. Austin: University of Texas Press.

Rabinow, Paul. 2008. *Marking time: On the anthropology of the contemporary*. Princeton, NJ: Princeton University Press.

———. 2011. *The accompaniment: Assembling the contemporary*. Chicago: University of Chicago Press.

Raihberg, G. E., and V. S. Shapik. 1966. *"Delo" Martensa*. Moscow: Politizdat.

Rees, Tobias. 2008. "Introduction: Today, what is anthropology." In *Designs for an anthropology of the contemporary*, edited by Paul Rabinow, George E. Marcus, James D. Faubion, and Tobias Rees, 1–12. Durham, NC: Duke University Press.

Richter, Jochen, and Axel Schmetzke. 2007. "Hugo Rheinhold's philosophizing monkey: A modern Owl of the Minerva." *NTM—International Journal of History and Ethics of Natural Sciences, Technology, and Medicine* 15 (2): 81–97.

Ricoeur, Paul. 1984. *Time and narrative*. Chicago: University of Chicago Press.

Rogers, Douglas. 2010. "Postsocialisms unbound: Connections, critiques, comparisons." *Slavic Review* 69 (1): 1–15.

Rosenberg, Daniel, and Anthony Grafton. 2010. *Cartographies of time*. New York: Princeton Architectural Press.

Rowlands, Michael. 1995. "Inconsistent temporalities in a nation state." In *Worlds apart: Modernity through the prism of the local*, edited by Daniel Miller, 23–42. London: Routledge.

Safonova, Tatiana, and István Sántha. 2013. *Culture contact in Evenki Land: A cybernetic anthropology of the Baikal Region*. Kent: Global Oriental.

Sahlins, Marshall. 1972. *Stone age economics*. Chicago: Aldine Publishing Company.

Sassen, Saskia. 2014. *Expulsions: Brutality and complexity in the global economy*. Cambridge, MA: Harvard University Press.

Scott, David. 2004. *Conscripts of modernity: The tragedy of colonial enlightenment*. Durham, NC: Duke University Press.

Scott, James. 1998. *Seeing like a state: How certain schemes to improve the human conditions have failed*. New Haven, CT: Yale University Press.

Sergeev, Mikhail A. 1955. *Nekapitalisticheskii Put' Razvitiia Malykh Narodov Severa*. Moscow: Izdatel'stvo AN SSSR.

Shove, Elisabeth, Frank Trentmann, and Richard Wilk, eds. 2009. *Time, consumption and everyday life: Practice, materiality, and culture*. Oxford: Berg.

Shubina, Tatiana. 2006. "Skul'pturnaia Kompozitsia 'Eritis Sigut Deus': Podarok V.I.leninu ot Amerikanskogo Biznessmena A. Hammera, Oktiabr' 1921 g." In *Dary Vozhdiam/Gifts to Soviet leaders*, edited by Nikolai Ssorin-Chaikov, 213. Moscow: Pinakotheke. Exhibition catalogue.

Sirina, A. A., and V. N. Davydov. 2017. "'Ne imeiuschie ni khlebopashestva, ni olenei, a odnu lish rechku etu': Peternalizm i Rynichnaia Ekonomika v Severo-Vostocjnom Pribaikalie." *Etnograficheskoe Obozrenie* 1:70–85.

Sorokin, Pitirim A., and Robert K. Merton. 1937. "Social time: A methodological and functional analysis." *American Journal of Sociology* 42 (5): 615–29.

Sosnina, Olga, and Nikolai Ssorin-Chaikov. 2001. "Facul'tet nenuzhnykh veschei: podarki dlia vozhdei." In *XX vek: Epokha, chelovek, vesch*, edited by Olga Sosnina, 132–47. Moscow: Novyi Indek.

———. 2009. "Postsocialism kak khronotop: post-sovetskaia publika na vystavke "dary vozhdiam." *Neprokosnovennyi Zapas* 64 (2): 207–26.

Ssorin-Chaikov, Nikolai. 2000. "Bear skins and macaroni: The social life of things at the margins of a Siberian state collective." In *The vanishing rouble: Barter networks and non-monetary transactions in post-Soviet societies*, edited by Paul Seabright, 345–61. Cambridge: Cambridge University Press.

———. 2003. *The social life of the state in subarctic Siberia*. Stanford, CA: Stanford University Press.

———. 2006a. "On heterochrony: Birthday gifts to Stalin, 1949." *Journal of Royal Anthropological Institute* 12 (2): 355–75.

———, ed. 2006b. *Dary Vozhdiam/Gifts to Soviet leaders*. Moscow: Pinakotheke. Exhibition catalogue.

———. 2013. "Gift/knowledge relations at the exhibition of gifts to Soviet leaders." *Laboratorium* 5 (2): 166–92.

———. 2016. "Soviet debris: Failure and the poetics of unfinished construction in Northern Siberia." *Social Research: An International Quarterly* 83 (3): 689–721.

———. 2017. "'Kupsty i inorogsty': sto let spustia: vvedenie." *Etnograficheskoe Obozrenie* 1:30–42.

Stirrat, R. L., and Heiko Henkel. 1997. "The development gift: The problem of reciprocity in the NGO world." *Annals of the American Academy of Political and Social Science* 554:66–80.

Stoler, Ann Laura. 2010. *Along the archival grain: Epistemic anxieties and colonial common sense*. Princeton, NJ: Princeton University Press.

Strathern, Marilyn. 1991. *Partial connections*. Savage, MD: Rowman & Littlefield.

Thompson, Edward P. 1967. "Time, work-discipline, and industrial capitalism." *Past and Present* 38:56–97.

Tsing, Anna. 2000. "The global situation." *Cultural Anthropology* 15 (3): 327–60.

Tumarkin, Nina. 1987. *Lenin lives!: The Lenin cult in Soviet Russia*. Cambridge, MA: Harvard University Press.

Ulturgasheva, Olga. 2012. *Narrating the future in Siberia: Childhood, adolescence, and autobiography among young Eveny*. Oxford: Berghahn.

Uvachan, V. N. 1984. *Gody Ravnye Vekam: Stroinel'Stvo Sotsializma Na Sovetskom Severe*. Moscow: Mysl'.

Verdery, Katherine. 1991. "Theorizing socialism: A prologue to the transition." *American Ethnologist* 18 (3): 419–39.

———. 1996. *What was socialism, and what comes next?* Princeton, NJ: Princeton University Press.

Viveiros de Castro, Eduardo. 1998. "Cosmological deixis and Amerindian perspectivism." *Journal of the Royal Anthropological Institute* 4 (3): 469–88.

Walker, John. 1974. *Self-portrait with donors: Confessions of an art collector*. Boston: Little, Brown.

Weinberg, Steve. 1992. *Armand Hammer: The untold story*. London: Abacus.

Wengrow, David. 2005. "Kingship, revolution and time: Perspectives on materiality and modernity." In *The qualities of time: Anthropological approaches*, edited by Wendy James and David Mills, 137–51. Oxford: Berg.

White, Hayden V. 1973. *Metahistory: The historical imagination in nineteenth-century Europe*. Baltimore: Johns Hopkins University Press.

Yanagisako, Sylvia Junko, and Carol Delaney, eds. 1995. *Naturalizing power: Essays in feminist cultural analysis*. New York: Routledge.

Yurchak, Alexei. 2006. *Everything was forever until it was no more: The last Soviet generation*. Princeton, NJ: Princeton University Press.

———. 2015. "Bodies of Lenin: The hidden science of communist sovereignty." *Representations* 129 (1): 116–57.

Zaloom, Caitlin. 2006. *Out of the pits: Traders and technology from Chicago to London*. Chicago: University of Chicago Press.

Zhirnov, Evgenii. 2000. "Na kogo rabotal tovarisch Armand." *Kommersant [newspaper]* 30 September.

Name Index

Alexievich, Svetlana, 81
Althusser, Louis, 99, 100
Anderson, Benedict, 14, 60
Auerbach, Erich, 14

Badiou, Alain, 47, 82
Bakhtin, Mikhail, 9, 16, 53, 72–74, 87, 92
Barbusse, Henri, 28, 53, 54
Baudelaire, Charles-Pierre, 122, 127
Baudrillard, Jean, 115, 116
Benjamin, Walter, 14
Bergson, Henri, 12–16
Boellstorff, Tom, 14, 76, 126, 127
Bourdieu, Pierre, 46, 72
Briggs, Jean, 78
Bruk, Mikhail, 42, 49, 50, 52, 55
Bulgakov, Mikhail, 36

Conrad, Sebastian, 3, 123

Derrida, Jacques, 46, 63, 128

Engels, Friedrich, 2, 11, 98

Fabian, Johannes, 11, 12, 33, 34, 127

Gell, Alfred, 15, 16, 33, 45, 52, 59

Giddens, Anthony, 122
Gramsci, Antonio, 66
Greenhouse, Carol, 4, 62
Groys, Boris, 28
Guyer, Jane, 126, 129

Haraway, Donna, 55, 93
Hattori, Tomohisa, 100
Hobbes, Thomas, 2, 17, 34, 95, 98, 101–108, 114, 115, 119
Hodges, Mark, 45, 76, 126

Joyce, James, 70, 76

Koselleck, Reinhart, 122–124, 127

Lafitau, Joseph-François, 91, 92
Latour, Bruno, 73, 93
Lefebvre, Henri, 44

Malinowksi, Bronislaw, 91, 121, 127
Marcus, George, 73–75, 121, 125–127
Marx, Karl, 2, 10, 11, 44, 48, 53, 97, 98, 114–116, 118, 122, 130
Massey, Doreen, 12, 130
Mauss, Marcel, 11, 12, 46, 60, 97, 98, 100–108, 112, 115
McTaggart, A. M. E., 15

Morgan, Lewis Henry, 97
Munn, Nancy, 6, 73, 122

Nielsen, Morten, 29, 30, 75, 88

Osharov, Mikhail, 99

Parry, Jonathan, 98
Payne, Robert, 118
Pedersen, Morten, 29, 30, 88
Propp, Vladimir, 16
Pushkin, Alexander, 6, 34

Rabinow, Paul, 75, 82, 88, 126, 127
Rees, Tobias, 75, 126
Rheinhold, Hugo Wolfgang, 1, 49
Rousseau, Jean-Jacques, 104

Sahlins, Marshall, 100–104, 106

Scott, James, 23, 25
Sergeev, Mikhail, 24
Shklovski, Victor, 16
Sosnina, Olga, 74, 87, 90, 117
Stoler, Ann, 31, 99

Thompson, E. P., 122
Tsing, Anna, 125

Uvachan, Vasilii Nikolaievich, 99

Verdery, Katherine, 4, 28, 61, 67, 84, 122, 123, 128, 129

Wells, H. G., 52, 60

Yurchak, Alexei, 8, 25, 28, 53

Zasulich, Vera, 97

Subject Index

American communists, 63
    US Communist party, 47, 61
anthropology of knowledge, 93
asbestos mining, 47

Bergsonian duration, 12–13, 73–75
Bolshevism (Bolsheviks), 5, 24, 53,
    97, 130
bureaucracy, 25, 34–36, 44, 58, 122

capital, 20, 43, 47, 48, 57, 65, 67, 114,
    115, 130
causality, 62, 104
charity, 98, 103, 108
Chernomyrdin, Victor, 28
china (sets), 85, 110–114
Christianity, 3, 9, 15, 29
    Christian conversion, 29, 35, 106
    Christian missions, 37
    Christian temporality, 7
Civil War (Russian), 23, 43, 59, 61, 64,
    65, 118
Cold War, 6, 55
collective farms, 20, 21, 31, 77, 81, 89
collectivization (Soviet), 21, 23, 118
Comintern, 24, 47
Communism, 24, 28, 56, 61, 64–66,
    97, 130

Communist Party, 5, 28, 42, 47, 56, 65,
    117, 130
concessions, 4, 48, 57–59, 62, 65, 67
consent, 71, 100–102
contract, 41, 62, 98, 100–104, 114

development, 25–26, 28–29, 32–33,
    35–37, 57, 81, 84–85, 86, 98, 100, 106,
    124–125, 129
    developmental hierarchy, 100
    developmental time, 16, 21–25, 27,
        30–32, 34–35, 71, 106
diary, 17, 69, 70, 72, 73, 88
double time, 100
drought/famine, 39, 40, 42, 43, 48, 56,
    57

Ekaterinburg, 40, 41, 47, 56
Evenki, the, or the Tungus, 8, 17,
    19–21, 23, 25–28, 30, 32, 34, 35,
    70–73, 77–84, 88, 95, 99, 106, 128,
    129
exchange, 9–11, 14–17, 26, 36, 37,
    44–46, 49, 56–58, 64, 66–68, 73, 86,
    90, 92, 96, 108, 121, 128
    commodity exchange, 42
    see gift exchange
    Marxist exchange, 10–11, 44

Fordism, 4, 59, 130
free will, 104

geodesic towers, 81
gift, 2–6, 9–11, 14, 17, 24, 25, 33, 35, 37,
    42–60, 62–64, 66–68, 72, 85–87,
    89, 91, 93, 95–108, 111–119, 121, 123,
    128–130
    gift credit, 43, 99, 100
    gift effects, 43
    gift exchange, 57
    gift time, 3, 42, 44, 45, 46–47, 49,
        67, 96, 98–101, 111, 121
    see Maussian gift theory
globalization, 85, 124, 125
Gorbachev, Mikhail, 71
gratitude, 9, 42, 57–59, 87, 98–101,
    104–108, 111, 114, 116

Hammer, Armand, 2–4, 8–11, 17, 37,
    39–45, 47–53, 55–64, 66–68, 74, 86,
    112, 113, 117, 130
    gift of pencils, 47, 52
    gift of surgical equipment, 39, 42,
        56, 59, 66
    gift of the figurine, 1–3, 9, 25, 42,
        53, 74
    gift of wheat flour, 41–42, 48,
        50–52
hau, 102, 103, 112
Hermitage, the, 48, 64, 76, 112
Hobbesian contract, 100, 101
Hobbesian gift, 101, 106, 123, 129
Hobbesian state of nature, 106
Hobbesian time(lessness), 106, 129
Hoover, J. Edgar, 47
humanitarianism, 47, 51, 57, 67, 98
    see development
hunting, 20, 21, 23, 26, 27, 31, 32, 77, 82,
    85, 95

iron logic, 63, 119

Katonga, 19–22, 25, 26, 28, 30, 31, 35,
    36, 70, 71, 74, 79, 84, 86–88, 106
Khalturun, Stepan, 118
Kremlin, 2, 3, 17, 42, 48–53, 57, 59, 66,
    83, 90, 91, 117, 118
    Museum of Lenin's Kremlin Flat,
        the, 48, 52, 53, 66

labor, 10, 11, 44, 65, 97, 114–116
    labor market, 114–115
    labor time, 10, 11, 44
    labor value, 44, 114
    see work
"Lenin," Vladimir, 8–9, 16, 19, 25, 30,
    32, 34, 36, 69–70, 72, 83–85, 86, 95,
    106, 128–129
    Arsen, 70, 80–81, 83
    Nadezhda, 19, 21, 70, 83–84
Lenin, Vladimir, 2–5, 8–10, 17, 19,
    23–25, 37, 42–44, 47–62, 64–68, 74,
    86, 98, 110–112, 115–119, 128–130
Leviathan, 28, 29, 35, 102, 103, 106

market, 2, 4, 10, 11, 17, 20, 26, 41–46,
    48, 49, 57, 58, 60, 67, 68, 80, 84, 85,
    114, 115, 126
    see labor market
Martens, Ludvig, 43, 55, 56, 60–64, 68
Marxism, 2, 3, 9–11, 15, 109, 112, 115, 130
    Marxist-Leninism, 130
    vernacular Marxism, 109–115
Maussian gift theory, 46–47, 59,
    96–98, 100, 102–103, 115–119
mining, 47, 55, 57
modernity, 2–4, 8–11, 14, 15, 17, 25, 36,
    59, 60, 64, 68, 72, 75, 76, 78, 81, 83,
    84, 92, 93, 96, 98–101, 105, 111, 118,
    119, 121–130
Mongolia, 24
Moscow, 6, 8, 17, 19, 39, 41, 43, 50, 52,
    54, 56, 58, 64, 71, 74, 79, 80, 83, 84,
    90, 117

multiplicity,
    cultural multiplicity, 12
    of gifts, 49
    temporal multiplicity, 6–9, 11, 15,
       16, 44, 45, 96, 108, 122, 123, 126

nationalization, 64
New Economic Policies, 4, 43, 55, 60,
    65–67
newtime, 122–125, 130
Nil, 29, 34, 36
Nizhnaia Tunguska River, 21, 96, 101
nomadism, 22, 23, 27, 84

"old" Nikolai, 69, 70, 72, 79, 83, 84, 86,
    88, 90
Ovid, 29, 34

peace, 55, 100, 102, 104–107, 115
perestroika, 128
perspectivism, 108
Petrograd, 43, 53, 56, 60
privatization, 32–33

reciprocity, 3, 13, 46, 59, 60, 67, 98, 100,
    103, 105, 107
reindeer herding, 19, 20–23, 27, 31–32,
    71, 77–78, 80
Russian Revolution, the, 61, 64
    February Revolution, the, 53
    October Revolution, the, 3–4, 52
Russian Soviet Government Bureau,
    61, 63, 64

Siberia, 19, 34, 36, 37, 73, 81, 85, 90, 92,
    96, 101, 109, 112, 114, 123, 128
simultaneity, 7, 8, 11–14, 36
Soviet Life, 49, 51
Soviet Russia, 7, 9, 10, 24, 39, 43, 44,
    48, 50, 55, 58–60, 62, 63, 66, 97
    Soviet distributive economy, 84
    Soviet "dreamworld," 53, 55

Soviet reform, 23–24, 84, 99
Soviet state, the (*see* the state)
speed, 41, 43, 47, 66, 75, 76, 124
    paradox of speed, the, 76
Stalin, Joseph, 6, 28, 87, 110–113, 116
state, the (Soviet), 21, 26, 27, 41, 44, 49,
    64, 67, 68, 71, 72, 73, 74, 78, 81–82,
    86–89, 91–93, 97, 98, 100
St. Petersburg (see Petrograd), 53, 60

temporalization, 46, 123–125, 127–130
time, 1–4, 6–17, 20–37, 39–49, 51–53,
    55–69, 71–84, 86–88, 91–93, 96–101,
    104–111, 115, 121–130
    chronotope, 9, 16, 21, 53, 72–74, 76,
       77, 82, 87, 91–93
    chronological time, 4, 8, 45, 49, 51,
       75, 123
    see gift time
    see labor time
    state time, 17, 45, 49, 58, 67, 72–73,
       78–79, 83, 88, 92, 129
    temporality of explanations, 71
    temporality of decisions, 71
    see temporalization
Tungus, the (*see* the Evenki), 19, 21,
    27, 29, 34, 95, 96, 99, 114
Turkestan, 24

Ulysses, 70
Urals, the, 40, 41, 43, 47, 48, 50, 56, 57,
    59, 62, 64, 110–112, 117
utopia, 66

war, 2, 6, 23, 24, 43, 55, 59–61, 64–66,
    71, 79, 81, 86, 101–108, 115, 118
War Communism, 64–66
warrior's mitten, the, 109–114, 116, 117
work, 4, 20, 27, 29, 31–33, 36, 61, 77–82,
    84, 86–87, 115, 123, 128
    see labor
    work day, 77

work time, 61, 77–78

working class, 24, 48, 52, 61, 97, 114–115, 117, 130

Workers' and Peasants' Inspectorate, 58

World Revolution, 63, 64, 66

World War I, 24, 60

World War II, 71, 79, 86

Yenisei river basin, 19, 21–22, 96

HAU Books is committed to publishing the most distinguished texts in classic and advanced anthropological theory. The titles aim to situate ethnography as the prime heuristic of anthropology, and return it to the forefront of conceptual developments in the discipline. HAU Books is sponsored by some of the world's most distinguished anthropology departments and research institutions, and releases its titles in both print editions and open-access formats.

www.haubooks.com

Supported by

Hau-N. E. T.
Network of Ethnographic Theory

University of Aarhus – EPICENTER (DK)
University of Amsterdam (NL)
Australian National University – Library (AU)
University of Bergen (NO)
Brown University (US)
California Institute of Integral Studies (US)
University of Campinas (BR)
University of Canterbury (NZ)
University College London (UK)
University of Cologne – The Global South Studies Centre (DE)
and City Library of Cologne (DE)
University of Colorado Boulder Libraries (US)
Cornell University (US)
University of Edinburgh (UK)
The Graduate Institute – Geneva Library (CH)
University of Groningen (NL)
Harvard University (US)
The Higher School of Economics in St. Petersburg (RU)
Humboldt University of Berlin (DE)
Indiana University Library (US)
Johns Hopkins University (US)
University of Kent (UK)
Lafayette College Library (US)
London School of Economics and Political Science (UK)
Institute of Social Sciences of the University of Lisbon (PL)
Ludwig Maximilian University of Munich (DE)
University of Manchester (UK)
The University of Manchester Library (UK)
Max-Planck Institute for the Study of Religious and Ethnic
Diversity at Göttingen (DE)
Musée de Quai Branly (FR)
Museu Nacional – UFRJ (BR)
Norwegian Museum of Cultural History (NO)
University of Oslo (NO)
University of Oslo Library (NO)
Princeton University (US)
University of Rochester (US)
SOAS, University of London (UK)
University of Sydney (AU)
University of Toronto Libraries (CA)

www.haujournal.org/haunet